A Parent's Guide to Graduate Jobs

How to help your child get a job after uni

Paul Redmond

A Parent's Guide to Graduate Jobs: How to help your child get a job after uni

This edition first published in 2012 by Trotman Publishing, an imprint of Crimson Publishing Ltd, Westminster House, Kew Road, Richmond, Surrey TW9 2ND

© Trotman Publishing 2011

Author: Paul Redmond

British Library Cataloguing in Publication Data
A catalogue record for this book is available from the British Library

ISBN 978 1 84455 395 2

Typeset by IDSUK (DataConnection) Ltd
Printed and bound in the UK by Ashford Colour Press, Gosport, Hants

Contents

Contents

About the author

D r Paul Redmond is head of Careers and Employability at the University of Liverpool and is one of the country's leading experts on generations and the graduate labour market. An experienced writer, author and speaker, he also presents at numerous events around the world.

Paul is the author of several books, including the best-selling *The Graduate Jobs Formula* (Trotman, 2010) and *Getting it right: A recruiter's guide to getting the best graduates* (Management Books, 2011).

Acknowledgements

I would like to thank everyone who has helped me with this book. At Crimson Publishing, Alison Yates helped develop the initial idea and backed it up with lots of advice and support, and Beth Bishop worked tirelessly and patiently in organising the text and making sure that it was practical and accessible to *real* parents.

For use of the tables and survey data, I would like to thank Martin Birchall at High Fliers Research. I would also like to thank the many graduate recruiters, HR managers and senior executives who kindly spent time with me discussing the new role of parents in the graduate job market.

Finally, I would like to thank the students and staff at the University of Liverpool for their ongoing help, support and inspiration.

This book is dedicated with much love and gratitude to my own personal 'helicopter parents', Michael and Jacqueline Redmond.

Introduction

Since 2008 the world of graduate jobs has been transformed. Before the credit crunch, job markets for graduates were plentiful and buoyant. On campuses up and down the country employers competed with one another to attract the best students. A 'War for Talent' was raging and students called the shots.

Today, that world has vanished. Job markets for graduates have shrunk by at least a quarter, leading to rising competition and a growing chasm between winners and losers. The 'War for Talent' is over – it's been won conclusively by employers. No longer do firms have to compete with one another for students: everyone knows there are more than enough job-seekers to go round to fill their vacancies many times over. If today's post-crunch employers *do* have a problem it's trying to secure the resources to sift through the mountains of application forms and CVs generated by every job vacancy.

As a university careers practitioner and writer I'm regularly contacted by parents of teenage and young adult children who are desperate for advice on graduate jobs and careers. Many are daunted by the sheer scale of the decisions which they and their children are required to take. With reduced (or often non-existent) support available from schools or local Connexions services, few families know where to turn to for the sort of expert help and insight that they seek. As a result, the process of career decision-making is made even more fraught and stressful than it already is.

Trying to remedy this advice gap has been one of the reasons for writing this book. I want to try to answer some of the many questions that parents and students ask me at university open days and other national careers events – questions which call desperately for answers.

A graduate careers guide ...
for *parents*

This book aims to put you in the shoes of today's student job-hunters as they compete in the world's toughest graduate job market. You'll discover a world of Saturday morning telephone interview (tip: always wear a suit), and hour-long psychometric tests.

At times, you might think some of what you're reading is far-fetched – an exaggerated version of *The Apprentice*. Trust me; none of this is made up. Before the crunch, all you had to do if you were a graduate to get a job was fill in an application form or submit a CV, then turn up for the interview. Today, that's just for starters. Most leading recruiters now require students to go through an extensive programme of 'Weapons of Mass Rejection': IQ tests, observed assessments, group presentations and, finally, a series of one-to-one and group interviews.

In some firms, the selection process now takes the best part of a year. Students are assessed not only on their academic skills but increasingly on their 'positional capital' – how they talk, look and perform in formal and 'informal' social contexts. So competitive is the process of recruitment and selection that the majority of applicants will never get beyond the first stage (which is, of course, the idea).

Three or four years of study, £20,000–£30,000 worth of debt and you don't even make it to an interview!

This book aims to help you give your child a fighting chance in the job market by showing you how the graduate job market operates. But don't expect it to be straightforward or even particularly rational. Today's graduate job market is a world in which rarely is anything quite as it seems; a world obsessed by 'talent' and social capital; a world in which the right experience and contacts go further than innate intelligence. A world you as a parent have to understand.

The journey to the graduate job market is full of obstacles – an almost continuous process of assessments and evaluations that begin well into a child's secondary schooling. This book has been written to accompany you on this journey – a journey few parents have undertaken before.

As we travel on this journey, you'll discover how the job market *really* works – its hidden secrets, in-built biases and informal 'rules' of engagement. You'll encounter leading graduate recruiters as they talk candidly and openly about what they expect from successful applicants; you'll also have a chance to look at the job market from the perspective of students, careers advisers, newly employed graduates and HR managers. As you'll see, each has their own unique perspective on what it takes to be not just employed, but employable.

A snapshot of today

Since the credit crunch, the world of graduate recruitment has been turned on its head. Applications to leading graduate recruiters have spiralled, generating incredible numbers and ratios. Consider, for example, the following snippets of information gleaned from the 2011 graduate recruitment market.

Jobs vs applications

	Jobs on offer	No. of applications received
Microsoft	100	110,000
RBS	40	35,000 – 40,000
HSBC	100	100,000
Co-operative	16	2,500

The number of applications sent to *Google* or *Apple*? Don't even go there.

Nationally, we estimate that around 80 graduates are competing for every 'graduate' job. 〞

In some sectors, this is a conservative estimate. Take the media, for example. Last year it was estimated that organisations such as the BBC and Channel 4 were receiving more than 250 applications for every graduate job.

Now pause for a moment and consider what life must be like for recruiters working at one of these top-brand employers. Each application consists of between 3,000–5,000 words. That means the minimum time spent processing each online application has to be around two hours. Two hours for over 100,000 applications. And all for just 100 jobs! No wonder that many graduate recruiters are thinking very seriously about the future of their recruitment programmes. To put it bluntly, they have no choice. Few organisations can afford the sheer staff resources to process this many applications. Not only is it too expensive, it's wildly inefficient. Unless something changes some of the leading graduate recruiters will have no choice but to pull out of the recruitment market. Either that or they'll go out of business.

The graduate job market isn't just struggling to cope with record levels of competition; in some places, the situation is threatening to go into full-scale meltdown.

Where you come in

Once, prior to the credit crunch, for some parents a book like this might have appeared unnecessary.

Not any more. So competitive has today's post-crunched graduate job market become that the role of the parent has started to change. No longer can parents afford to watch neutrally from the touchline.

When a child's future is at stake, for most parents, the stakes are simply too high.

So it's no wonder that across the UK parents are resorting to direct action – taking first-hand responsibility for managing and guiding their child's career. Invariably they'll tell you they have to, that they have no choice. That if they don't do it, who will?

Only now is the importance of parents in the graduate job market being recognised. As a parent, there are a number of key contributions you can make to give your child a head start in the graduate job market. This book will reveal to you what these contributions are, and how to use them to the best effect.

Once, parents left their child's career planning in the hands of paid experts. Today, they're taking on the responsibility for themselves.

If this sounds like you, congratulations: you've just got yourself a new job.

But how far should you go?

A few years ago, I wrote an article for a national newspaper about a new phenomenon I'd observed taking place in university careers fairs: small groups of smartly dressed men and women moving confidently and purposefully between exhibition stands. Some were chatting to recruiters, others were busy gathering up armfuls of brochures. Too old to be students, too organised to be window-shoppers, far too well-dressed to be academics, something about the behaviour of these people urged me to find out more. Who were they and what were they doing at a university careers fair? The answer amazed me: they were *parents*.

Hard as it now is to credit it, but in 2007 the idea of parents attending student careers fairs was sufficiently shocking enough to make national headlines. Why? Because until then, it was widely assumed that once you went to university, as far as parental influence was concerned, you were on your own: a free agent, out of reach of parental tentacles. The arrival of parents at careers fairs proved this was no longer the case.

At some level, the article must have resonated with people, because it went viral, appearing in newspapers, magazines, TV current affairs programmes not just in the UK but across the world.

What grabbed most of the headlines was the phrase 'helicopter parent' – a term I coined to describe a particular category of parents who seemed to 'hover' over the lives, education and careers of their twenty-something children. Though slightly tongue-in-cheek, my aim was to get across the point that in both formal and tertiary education parents were assuming ever greater responsibility for their child's careers. Parents were doing it for themselves, literally, taking on roles and responsibilities once reserved exclusively for teachers and careers advisers.

And the key point was this: *it actually worked.*

Since then I've discovered parents hovering over lots of other careers and education-related activities. In schools and sixth-form colleges the presence of parents is greater than ever. Even in higher education – once the ultimate parent-free zone – parental involvement is becoming much more common.

But being a helicopter parent is one thing. Being an *effective* helicopter parent is a different thing altogether. Any parent can hover, make lots of noise, generate their own gales of hot air. What counts is knowing when and where to intervene and how to make your presence felt. It's also about knowing the boundaries. Some parents assume so much responsibility for their child's education and career planning that, from an employer's perspective, it becomes counter-productive. See our advice on p243 for how to be an *effective* helicopter parent.

Parents – an employer's perspective

While researching this book, I have spoken to numerous high-profile graduate recruiters. Most reported increased incidents of parents contacting them on behalf of their son or daughter.

While most of these contacts were benign, some were far more controversial. One senior manager based in a top professional services firm told me how, after making several job offers, parents had been in touch with her to try to renegotiate their son or daughter's starting salary. In her words:

> ❝ I felt as if I were negotiating with a footballer's agent – someone who was acting on behalf of their client. Only in this instance, the 'client' was their child. ❞
>
> HR manager, professional services firm

Another employer – HR director at one of the UK's most prestigious graduate recruiters – spent an hour with me berating parents who did everything for their children, before apologising and dashing off to pick up her 22-year-old son's passport from the Post Office. Employers too are parents, many of them of the helicopter variety.

Of course, this is to be expected. As we have seen, parents now play a much more active role in students' decision-making processes, whether the decision is which A levels to take, which universities to attend or which job offers to accept. The hovering starts with the UCAS form and continues well beyond graduation.

It all comes down to balance. Some recruiters expressed concern that increased levels of parenting could reduce a graduate's self-motivation and reliability.

> ❝ One senior investment banker told me how, in her opinion, her firm's new recruits were unreliable – particularly when attending off-site meetings. Despite picking up starting salaries well in excess of £30,000, their attendance could never be guaranteed. ❞

But such responses were in the minority. Most recruiters were more stoical (after all, as parents themselves, many openly admitted to deploying the same tactics as students' parents were using with them). Most accepted that a generational shift has taken place, that in today's job market, the stakes and costs were noticeably higher than ever before. As such, it was to be expected that parents would become far more integral to the graduate recruitment process. In the battle to attract the best graduates, employers accept that parents have gone from being neutral observers to key professional advisers.

If you didn't know it already, you've just become a careers adviser.

About this book

This book has three aims:

1. To help you, as a parent, understand what it takes in today's post-crunched job market for a student (i.e. your son or daughter) to get a good job.

2. To give a first-hand, insider's view into how the graduate job market operates – its obstacles, conventions, and hidden rules.

3. To provide you with the information, advice, tactics and strategies to help your child plan and achieve their future career goals.

Think of this book as a user's guide to the graduate job market. As such, you'll find within it lots of information, advice and suggestions, all designed to help you prepare your child – whatever stage they are at – for entering the job market. Combine this with the right blend of strategies and tactics (all of which are covered in these pages) and your child will have a head start in the competition for graduate jobs.

To help you understand how graduate job markets now work, the book takes you behind the scenes, showing you what employers look for in applicants – what makes those who are successful stand out from those who aren't; which degrees offer the best job prospects; and what graduates have to do to get a job offer.

The book will also bring you up to date with what other parents are doing to give their children a positional advantage in the job market. You will discover, for example, how parents are increasingly harnessing their own networks, experiences and contacts to trade internships amongst their friends; how parents are playing a greater role in the graduate job market; and how, as consumers, parents are exerting a greater influence in the world of education.

❝ Once, all parents had to do was shuttle students to and from university. Now they're following them inside the gates. ❞

Employability

During the book, I use the word 'employability' a fair bit. Since the economic downturn, employability has become one of the most important and influential ideas in higher education. Once, universities focused on helping students become employed. Today, however, the emphasis is on helping students acquire the skills, attitudes and knowledge to be able to manage their careers on an ongoing basis. That's essentially what employability is: the ability to be able to manage your own career.

How the book is structured

The book sets out to answer the type of questions parents frequently ask at university open days, careers fairs and other employer-related events. As such, I hope you find the book is directly relevant to your own situation.

The book has four parts:

Part 1 A parent's guide to the 21st century graduate job market

We start with an overview of the post-credit crunch graduate job market. Rather than just setting out the economic trends and data, I have tried to give you a personal insight into what it's like to be a graduate recruiter – what it's like to have 9,000 job applications in your in-tray.

We also look at what it now takes to make students employable – the skills, experiences, aptitudes and attitudes that mark out the successful from the unsuccessful. As you'll see, as far as many recruiters are concerned, academic excellence is now increasingly taken as a given; what stands out is what students do in their 'spare' time – and part of that time they'll spend with you. This means that as a parent, you have a substantial and long-term opportunity to influence your child's future. That is, as long as you know what you're doing.

In the final chapter I make some bold predictions about the future of the graduate job market – the shifts that experts predict will revolutionise both the world and the job market.

Part 2 Planning for university

In Part 2 we look in detail at higher education and how it relates to the job market. Here you'll discover if it's really worth paying for your child to go to uni, and how the subject your child studies at uni, or indeed how where they study, affects their chance of getting a graduate job.

We'll look at what universities are doing to boost students' employability: with the rise in tuition fees, what are universities doing to help your child get a job once they graduate? I'll arm you with the questions you should be asking to ensure you are getting value for your money.

Part 3 During university: eyes on the prize

Part 3 looks closely at what your son or daughter should be doing when at university to give themselves a head start in the job market. We'll show you why, when it comes to getting a graduate job it's not just academic achievements that count but, increasingly, the skills and experiences gained by your child in their spare time.

With the prospect of rising student debt, it's essential that students make the most of university. This section looks at what your child can do during uni to make them stand out from the crowd, including the role of extra-curricular achievements, work experience, gap years and internships.

Part 4 Getting that job

Finally, Part 4 explores the tactics your child will need to actually get that job after uni. We consider in detail how you as a parent can help your child succeed – and that means understanding how it all works. As well as talking you through the process of applications, CVs, interviews and assessment centres, we'll look at some key advice from employers themselves.

We end with an employability timeline, helping you plan and prepare for the critical events and opportunities that exist (often invisibly) in every student's timetable.

> **"** Whatever stage your child is now at – be it preparing for university, or desperately trying to get on the career ladder – this book will give you

the knowledge and advice you need to help your child compete in a competitive market, and land themselves a job. **"**

Task

As you read, you'll notice a series of tasks for you to either think about or accomplish. These tasks have been designed to help you reflect on your own career, your role as a parent, and how you and your child can combine your joint skills, experience, insights and enthusiasm to maximum effect in the job market. Who knows – you might even find it gives you a chance to think about your own career and ambitions.

Part 1

A parent's guide to the 21st century graduate job market

Part 1 provides you with a brief introduction to the world of work – not just any work: graduate work. It reveals how the psychological contract between employers and employees has been rewritten, and shows you why your child's career will be very different from your own.

You'll discover the four types of graduate jobs; how these relate to one another, and the forces which are reshaping post-crunch economies.

We'll also touch on the world of 'employability' – the buzz word that is the key to graduate success.

1
The new world of work

Over the past few years, the world of work has changed beyond recognition. Gone are the old certainties that characterised the pre-credit crunch economy. Not only are jobs today less secure, they're subject to ever-accelerating forces of change. The combined forces of globalisation, technology and changing demographics are transforming the workplace.

From an employment perspective, organisations in both the public and private sectors have seen widespread changes. Companies have become flatter, with layers of middle-management stripped out entirely or outsourced to other organisations (frequently located overseas). At the same time, new technology has enabled work practices to be transformed. Once, people were given the responsibility and time to develop their own specialism. Today, it's common practice for people to work in multi-disciplinary teams where specialists are replaced by groups of people working together to solve short-term projects.

All these changes are having a profound impact on jobs and careers. Gone are the days of the 'job for life', the upwardly mobile career path, the guaranteed pay increments, carriage clocks and gilt-edged pension schemes. All these benefits were brought to an abrupt end with the credit crunch. In their place has emerged a new and aggressive marketplace consisting of *customers* and *clients*.

❝ Employers are now customers; employees the salespeople. Employees used to work for their employers, often for life. From now on, they'll work with them – for as long as they're needed. ❞

The characteristics of this marketplace are clear to see: short-term contracts, endemic job insecurity, digitisation, global competition and multiple career paths. Once, it was possible to plan and manage your career. In the future, you'll only know what your career was when you look back at it when it's over.

For your child's generation, career planning will be like driving while looking through the rear-view mirror. We don't just need to teach them how to drive, we need to forget everything we have ever taken for granted about driving and learn a completely different way of doing it.

Eighty graduates for every job

For graduates, not only is the world of work that they'll enter into now relatively unknown but the route to the job market has also radically changed.

Before the crunch, graduate jobs were plentiful. Students could pick and choose between different organisations and different career paths. To make it easy for them, many university careers services and graduate recruiters held annual careers fairs, which, with their long aisles of exhibitors gradually came to be more like shopping malls than recruitment events. This may have been intentional: demand for graduates seemed insatiable. Each year, after staging hugely costly recruitment campaigns, some employers would recruit upwards of 1,000 graduates. Never was there a better time to be a graduate.

All changed, changed utterly. Graduates are still in demand, but the days of plenty are over.

❝ Competition is the new name of the game. Now, 80 graduates compete for every graduate job, and in some sectors the ratio is already considerably higher. **❞**

In larger universities, careers fairs and other recruitment events still take place every year and they still look like shopping malls. But after the credit crunch, these are shopping malls with a difference: now it's not the shoppers who make the purchasing decisions, but the shopkeepers. The power now rests with the employers, to be as discerning over their purchases as they wish to be.

Even graduate jobs themselves have changed. Traditional graduate jobs still exist, but not in sufficient numbers to keep pace with the supply of students entering the job market.

❝ In 2011, around 400,000 graduates completed their degrees and entered the job market. Awaiting them were approximately 20,000 'graduate' jobs. That the majority found work is testament to how rapidly the world of the graduate job market is changing – but doesn't necessarily sing of success. **❞**

Unfortunately, most graduates did not secure a job for which a degree qualification was required. One of the unfortunate by-products of the credit crunch has been the dramatic rise in the number of graduates working in non-graduate jobs (jobs for which degrees are usually not required). Such under-employment is a major risk for today's students. In a post-crunched job market, unemployment isn't always the biggest danger for graduates to be concerned about. It's being in a job for which you didn't have to go to university. In chapter 20, we look at ways of utilising this time, as a way of further developing your child's skills, should they find themselves in 'under-employment'.

End of the psychological contract

As the saying goes, if *being* in a crappy job isn't your fault, *staying* in a crappy job is. To survive and thrive in the new world of post-crunched work, your child will need to manage their own relationship with work.

This is easier said than done. After all, for much of the past century, careers were managed by employers – in return for the loyalty and commitment of the workers. This 'psychological contract' between workers and managers remained unbroken until the start of the 21st century. So enduring has it been for them, many parents still assume that it will apply to their own children's future careers. It won't. In organisations across the UK, Europe and the USA, it has already broken down.

The chart below is taken from a report by the Association of Graduate Recruiters that appeared towards the end of the 20th century. With great foresight, the authors predicted just how the psychological contract between employees and organisations would shift in the years ahead. The left-hand column lists the words and images that defined the 20th century world of work – 'ladders', 'career clarity', 'job', 'rising income and security' – and compares them to the images and concepts which are now defining today's world of work.

The new vocabulary of graduate careers

From	To
Ladders and escalators	Bridges
Career clarity	Fog
Employer	Customer
Job	Adding value
Functional identity	Project team role
Career	Portfolio
Progression	Personal growth
Rising income and security	Maintaining employability
Education and training	Lifelong learning

Source: AGR

This new 'psychological contract' between employers and employees will shape and define your child's career future. Whereas the old, 20th century contract was based on loyalty and security in return for a predictable and assured career path, today's contract is based on a market-driven, customer/client relationship characterised by short-term contracts, two-way flexibility and constant re-evaluation of where both parties stand. As one employer said:

> ❝ Careers used to be like formal dinners – set courses, planned menus, predictable sequences. Now they're like Chinese banquets: lots of variety, lots of choice and with no one 'best' way of doing things. ❞

The chart below is again from the AGR report. It illustrates how, with a new psychological contract in place, the 21st century job market differs from that of the 20th.

EMPLOYEE	The old contract	Interim – no contract	The new contract
Offers	skill and loyalty	skill and hard work	ability to learn
Wants	security and career	lifestyle and development	'employability' and quality of life

EMPLOYER	The old contract	Interim – no contract	The new contract
Wants	skill and loyalty	productivity or long hours	flexibility
Offers	security and career	a job	high pay or good experience

Change has come – and it's here to stay

As we have seen, changes in the psychological contract are demanding radically different ways of thinking about work, careers and what it takes to get a job. So fast are these changes happening that people can easily find themselves cut off, marooned in a world of confusion and out-of-date thinking. That's because in today's world of work, getting new ideas into your head isn't the problem; it's getting the old ideas out. Rarely is this a problem for young people – after all, because of their age, few will have known any alternative. But this definitely isn't the case for parents – in other words, you.

> ❝ As you will have started work in the 20th century – a time when a different psychological contract between employers and employees was in place – there's every danger that you could be accidentally preparing your child for a lost world of work that no longer exists. ❞

No parent consciously sets out to do this – to prepare their child for an out-of-date world of work. But this is exactly what happens when change takes place so fast. Keeping up to date is a full-time job.

So what will be the difference between you and your child's careers? How will your son or daughter's working life differ from yours?

Below are several reasons why your child's experience of work may turn out to be radically different from anything you've experienced in your own career.

Fewer gold watches

One of the consequences of the past decade has been the end of the 'job for life' mentality. They think it's all over? It is now. Over the course of your child's career, it's likely that job changes will become ever more frequent, with fewer people spending their entire working lives with one organisation.

It's not that people will suddenly become less loyal or committed to their jobs; rather, it'll be the other way around. Jobs will be less committed to the people paid to do them. All this will mean that the key skill that your child will have to acquire is the need to think flexibly: to make quick and easy transitions to new workplaces, new jobs, new teams. Fitting in will be more important than sticking it out.

Coping with uncertainty

All this is much easier said than done. As you'll probably know already from your own career, change has a habit of creating winners and losers. It's one thing to ask people to be comfortable with change and uncertainty, it's another thing when change and uncertainty involve your job. Change is rarely comfortable – particularly if imposed from outside. Fortunately, there's an antidote to this inevitable state of uncertainty: ongoing, lifetime learning.

For your child's generation, learning won't end with formal education, nor will it always come with a certificate or formal qualification. Learning, in the 21st century will be a lifelong pursuit, a process rather than a one-off event.

In the 20th century, once you were qualified, that was that. You had a job for life. Today, a qualification (even for a medical practitioner) has a shelf-life of five years, tops. After that, it's gathering dust. Your child's graduation ceremony won't be the end of their education; it's just the beginning.

We're all in it alone

Not just a lyric from a Grateful Dead song, but a wise commentary on a 21st century reality. The fact is, for many careers, the 20th century provided certain forms of protective support structures – job titles, job descriptions, work protocols, 'permanent' contracts of employment, even 'personnel departments'. Today, in case you hadn't noticed, there are no personnel departments, just 'human resources'. This isn't just a trendy change of titles but an indication of just how profoundly the psychological contract is re-engineering the workplace.

> " In the 20th century, employees were 'personnel' – unique, individual people. In the 21st century, they're 'resources' – to be moved around, downscaled, reprogrammed and, if needs be, shut down. "

As far as your child's career is concerned, this calls for a new psychological toughness – the ability to go it alone, to stand on one's own two feet and to not be dependent on anyone else. Self-reliance – the ability to go it alone – is the order of the day.

Flexibility and adaptability

As the pace of change gets ever hotter, more employers are demanding graduates who can demonstrate flexibility and adaptability.

As far as work is concerned, the idea of flexibility has a simple, straightforward meaning.

It's the ability to *adapt* and apply existing capabilities to new situations. In other words, we're talking about the transfer of skills from one situation to another. Think of it as like being an actor. Gone are the days when actors could spend a career lifetime performing nothing but Shakespeare. In today's media-driven world, actors need to be versatile: this week *Coriolanus*, next week *Coronation Street*.

Learning how to be your own publicist

One of the biggest differences between the 20th century workplace and that of the 21st is the need to be able to manage your own career: in other words, to handle your own relationship with the world of work. Many parents find that this is where their own career experience differs sharply with that of their child's.

In the 20th century, in return for loyalty, organisations (particularly those in the public sector) managed their employees' careers, offering them regular promotions, guaranteed salary and cost of living increments, job security and long-term stability.

Today, this managed work environment is fast breaking down. Graduates entering the 21st century workplace are often required to negotiate their own starting salary, manage their own training and development, oversee their own career moves and build their own networks. In a matter of a few short years, much of the architecture of support, which defined so much of last century's workplace, has been either scrapped or outsourced.

To stay employable, today's graduates need to be their own manager, publicist, PR agent, financial adviser and career coach. The problem is, as many graduates are already discovering, rarely are negotiations with employers conducted on a level playing field. This means that unless they know what they're doing, and how to negotiate effectively, there's a heightened risk that they'll be exploited. As we'll see, in today's post-crunched workplace, the exploitation of graduates is already well advanced.

> ❝ That's where you come in – stepping up to the plate to fill this role, if your child has either not grasped the situation or just needs a shove in the right direction . . . But before you're able to do this, make sure you're fully aware of the world you're coaxing your child into. ❞

Centuries apart

The problem most parents (and authors) face when thinking about the future job market is that we can't help thinking in the wrong century. Partly, it's inevitable. After all, nearly all of us were born, brought up, educated, and first employed in the 20th century. We might happen to live and work in the 21st century, but our hearts and minds are rooted firmly in the century before.

Already, however, it's clear that the 21st century is shaping up to be a very different century from its predecessor. In fact, it's as different as the 19th century was to the 20th – the difference between Elgar and Elvis, Disraeli and Dylan, Queen Victoria and Queen the rock band.

If anything, the differences are even greater. Consider, for example, the chart below.

20th century world	21st century world
Nation states call the shots	Global brands call the shots
Technology driven by business	Technology driven by consumers
Media organisations 'own' the news	Consumers 'make' the news, using digital handheld devices
Just in time communication	Real time communication
US dominant world power	BRIC countries (Brazil, Russia, India & China) set to assume dominance by end of century
Governments control information	Wikileaks
Highest example of technological achievement: lunar landings	Average desktop computer now has more IT power than NASA used to send astronauts to the Moon.

Digital immigrant meets digital native

Being from a different century is a problem, particularly when you're trying to advise and guide a generation that's about to spend its entire working life in a different century to you. Not only do you think differently, your world view is different.

Take technology, for example. According to social theorist Mark Prensky, the world is divided into two groups: digital immigrants and digital natives.

You can tell which one you are by the words you use to describe modern technology. That's because whereas digital natives have been born into a world of computers, laptops, cell phones and 24/7 communications, digital immigrants have had to teach themselves the language of digitisation – in effect, they've had to learn a new way of thinking about the world.

Mostly, digital immigrants have coped very well; there are times, however, when they let their guard down, when they lapse back in to the old ways. You can tell if someone's a digital immigrant by the way they say 'mobile phone' (tip: it's just a phone. Digital natives have never known telephones to be anything other than mobile).

Digital immigrants will also say things like 'digital camera' (for anyone born after 1980, it's just a camera); they'll also feel the need, when presented with a long email, to print it out before reading it. It's as if their minds haven't quite evolved yet to cope with online reading. But they're getting there!

There's a good chance that you and your child are classic digital immigrants and digital natives. Together, you're a powerful combination; but remember, the days of the digital immigrants are being rapidly replaced by the natives.

Think about your own career: how is today's world of work different from when you started working? What are some of the main differences? If you could go back in time and offer careers advice to your 21-year-old self, what would it be?

2
What is a graduate job?

As you read this chapter, you're about to encounter lots of terms and expressions containing the word 'graduate': 'graduate jobs', 'graduate employers', 'graduate job classifications' and, of course, 'graduates'.

arely do universities and recruiters take the time to explain what these terms mean. But what exactly *is* a graduate job? For that matter, what is a graduate?

Before we go any further, let's get a few things straight.

- **Graduate**: For the purposes of this book, a 'graduate' is a student who has successfully completed a university or college degree course. In the UK, most graduates will have studied at one of the country's 170 or so universities and colleges.

- **Student**: A student is someone who is studying towards a university qualification or programme. If a student is studying for a first degree, they're officially known as an *undergraduate*. A student who has completed a first degree course and enrolled on a higher degree is a *postgraduate*.

What *type* of graduate your child becomes is dependent on the letters they have after their names.

Depending on the subject of undergraduate study, graduates come in many different varieties – BA (Bachelor of Arts), B.Sc. (Bachelor of Science), B.Eng. (Bachelor of Engineering), LL.B. (Bachelor of Law), B.Ed. (Bachelor of Education) and so on.

Defining what's meant by the term 'graduate job' is slightly harder.

Once, 'graduate job' was a term used to describe any job for which a degree was an explicit requirement. But as the world of work has become more complex, leading to the creation of different types, defining what is and what isn't a 'graduate job' is no longer as straightforward as it once was.

The four types of graduate jobs

Graduate jobs come in four varieties:

Categories	Examples
Traditional	Lawyers, barristers, medics, architects, teachers
Modern	Business managers (public and private sector), engineers, accountants
New	Nurses, graphic designers, marketing managers
Niche	IT programmers, cartographers, animators

Source: Elias & Purcell

Traditional jobs

Examples of traditional jobs include dentists, doctors, lawyers, judges, architects and teachers: jobs for which degrees have always been an essential prerequisite.

Graduates entering 'traditional' graduate jobs will need to use their specific degree subject. They'll probably also have to meet professional standards laid down by professional organisations.

Working in a traditional graduate job confers lots of social and cultural benefits: it can also lead to above-average earnings. From this, vertical career progression can follow. But there's always a snag.

Acceptance into one of these jobs is usually extremely competitive. Not only do students need to convince recruiters that they possess the relevant academic skills and knowledge, they must also demonstrate that they have the right balance of personal skills and attributes. For traditional graduate jobs, what counts isn't just how clever you are, it's how well you fit in with the job's professional standards.

Modern jobs

This category encompasses business managers, engineers, army officers and accountants.

Modern graduate jobs are to be found in both the public and private sectors. They are also well known for not being as choosy as their traditional job counterparts about the subject of their degree. Ask 100 graduate business managers what they studied at university and you'll find they mention a broad spectrum of subjects – from biology to English literature (relatively few will actually have a degree in business studies).

> ❝ Rumour has it that roughly one in 10 graduates becomes a business manager: proof of both how large this sector of the job market has become and how graduates' career horizons aren't always as wide as you may think. ❞

As far as employers are concerned, many modern graduate jobs are located in professions which only in recent years have become populated by graduates. In the past, it might have been possible to enter these occupations without a degree. Today, however, it's becoming increasingly rare.

New jobs

Many 'new' graduate jobs have only appeared in the past decade or so. Again, like modern graduate jobs, entry to these jobs is increasingly dependent on a degree. No degree, no job offer.

New graduate jobs can often be found in areas such as administration, design, technical work and the caring professions (including nursing, which since 2010 has been a graduate-entry occupation).

Niche jobs

The final category of the graduate job market is the 'niche' sector. Niche jobs tend to fall in specialist areas in which graduates can often be found in small numbers. Many niche graduate jobs are to be found in small and medium-sized organisations. This category can also include self-employment.

These four categories of graduate jobs are a useful way of thinking about the graduate job market. It opens your mind to what possibilities await graduates.

The graduate job market doesn't just include the 'traditional' graduate jobs that everyone is aware of. It also includes new and niche occupations, such as graphic designers, human resource officers, planning executives, architects, airline pilots, civil engineers, retail managers and IT consultants.

Task

Think about what you consider to be a graduate job. Is your view too narrow?

What every graduate job has in common

While there may be very specific different types of graduate jobs, they all share qualities that group them under the same umbrella term.

In 2011, the Higher Education Careers Service Unit (HECSU) launched a survey to find what graduate jobs had in common with one another. In total, researchers spoke to just under 10,000 graduates. Their aim was to find out what made a 'graduate' job – the key components that set graduate jobs apart from others. The findings made for interesting reading.

Graduate jobs – regardless of whether they're 'traditional', 'modern', 'new' or 'niche' – offer five crucial and indivisible ingredients.

Autonomy

Unlike many other jobs, graduate jobs offer the potential for independent action and for managing your own workload.

Research shows that what graduates generally look for in a job is the chance to work autonomously and independently. This doesn't mean to say that graduates expect to be their own bosses; most graduates still expect to work for an organisation within a traditional management structure. But being able to take ownership of your own workload, to make your own decisions, is something that most graduates value very highly. And it's one of the best ways to identify a graduate job.

Responsibility

In addition to offering lots of autonomy, graduate jobs also provide lots of responsibility – often early on in a graduate's career.

Employers know that graduates are more likely to stay with them, and stay committed, if they feel that their skills and abilities are being recognised with additional responsibility. That is why many review graduates' career paths on an annual basis. It's also why some of the largest graduate recruiters like to move new recruits into positions of responsibility, often within their first year after university.

Contribution

One of the defining features of today's graduates is the desire to know they're making a contribution to their organisation. Not only does this provide graduates with a sense of professional satisfaction but it also enables them to feel more attuned to their employer's goals and objectives.

Impact

Linked to contribution, graduate jobs also focus on making an impact – either on the bottom line or in other, tangible, ways.

> Employers view graduate recruits as essential for the future direction and growth of their organisation. They're also a powerful conduit to tap in to new ideas and learning.

Creativity

Another feature which defines a graduate job is the opportunity for the job holder to be creative, to be able to think original thoughts and to pursue unconventional ideas. In a harsh job market and economic climate, creativity isn't usually the top priority that employers focus on when trying to ensure their organisation rides out the economic maelstrom.

Yet surveys show that firms that retain creativity at the heart of their businesses – despite pressures to abandon it for practices more attuned to austerity and caution – are often best placed to profit once the market starts to improve.

Creativity is one of the key reasons why employers recruit graduates. They might not have years of experience under their belts, but one thing graduates can offer business is creativity.

Where are the jobs?

Does where your child lives in the country affect their chance of getting a graduate job? Your child may have spoken of the need to 'move to London' after they graduate – as that's where all the jobs are. But is this the case?

The chart below illustrates how where you live affects your access to graduate job opportunities – particularly with some of the leading UK recruiters. What you can see makes for surprising reading. While the spread may look pretty even throughout the rest of the country, 86% of the top recruiting firms offer job vacancies in London. This is almost three times the proportion of jobs offered to graduates in Northern Ireland and more than double the number based in East Anglia.

So when your child suggests moving into a small flat in south London, instead of staying put in his university market town, there's a very good argument for it.

Geographical distribution of graduate vacancies at leading UK firms (2011)

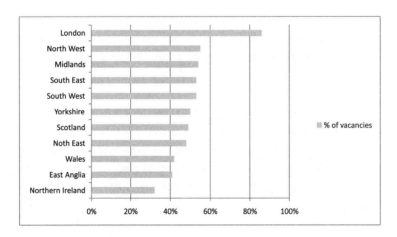

Source: Graduate prospects

❝ London remains without doubt the epicentre of recruitment activities. In 2011, an incredible nine out of 10 of the 100 biggest hirers were offering job vacancies in London, and a further half were planning to hire new recruits to work in the south-east of England. ❞

While this doesn't mean that all graduate jobs are situated around the M25 it does prove that almost every major graduate employer offers jobs within this region.

The north-west of England, the Midlands, and the south-west offer the next highest numbers of graduate recruiters, followed by Yorkshire and the north-east of England. Of all English regions, East Anglia appears to be the worst place to find graduate jobs.

According to graduate recruitment researcher High Fliers, in addition to offering vacancies in England, around 40% of recruiters were also offering vacancies in Scotland and Wales, while just over 32% were recruiting specifically in Northern Ireland.

Your child's chances of securing a graduate job are not restricted by geographical location, but as this data shows, where you live is never neutral. If your child lives, or wants to live, in an area with relatively fewer graduate recruiters, don't despair. Locations of graduate employers are relatively fluid, and as companies move locations the picture can change rapidly.

It's worth bearing in mind, however, that in order to maximise their employability, geographical mobility may be an option your child needs to consider, particularly in the early years of a career.

3

How graduate jobs have been affected by the recession

Much has been written about the economic downturn – or the 'credit crunch', as it was initially, and somewhat casually, named. But as the economy recovers, be it at snail's pace, there's no doubt the economic downturn has impacted on your child's future career prospects. What do you as a parent need to know about the crunch?

You always take the weather with you

The first thing you'll want to do before embarking on a journey is to check the weather forecast. As you know, in purely economic terms, the years since 2007 have made for stormy conditions. In fact, for many people, conditions have been nothing short of turbulent. It's to be expected then that this should have had a direct impact on graduate job markets, and it'll affect your child too.

For graduate jobs, the impact of the recession has been immediate and dramatic. Immediate, in terms of the number of large recruiters who either vanished (for example, Lehman Brothers), and dramatic in terms of how the recession was reported by the media. Much of the coverage was overblown: even at the height of the downturn, levels of graduate unemployment rarely approached the 12% recorded at the depths of 1992. Another reason why the downturn seemed so bad for graduates was that for much of the past decade things had been going so well. Jobs were plentiful, employers were competing to recruit the best and brightest graduates, and unemployment was below 5%. As far as many students and their parents were concerned, things had never been so good.

That's what made the Great Crunch of 2009 so memorable. Overnight, job vacancies for graduates plunged by 18%. The press had a field day, pronouncing the graduate job market to be in permanent decline. Too many graduates, competing for too few jobs, with the situation only bound to get worse. Fortunately, to borrow a phrase from Mark Twain, reports of the graduate job market's death were greatly exaggerated. Against many commentators' predictions, within a year the job market rallied and actually began to grow.

The changing graduate job market (2003-11)

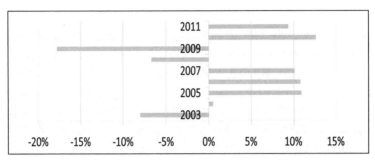

Source: High Fliers, 2011

By 2011, recruitment activity amongst many of the leading recruiters was back to pre-crunch levels. Even in the depths of recession, it seems that few were willing to take a chance on scaling back on graduate recruitment. Some even increased their intake, hoping against hope no doubt that once economic conditions improved such confidence would be rewarded.

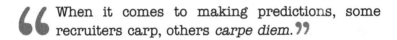 **When it comes to making predictions, some recruiters carp, others *carpe diem*.**

But don't assume this means there are enough jobs to go around. There aren't. Even though the top 100 firms are back in business, compared to the overall supply of graduates the overall number of jobs they have to offer is miniscule – a fact which for many is only now becoming apparent.

Hopefully these employers will have email accounts with lots of spare computing capacity, because as many have discovered, once the message gets out that you are known as a recruiting organisation, you can expect to receive lots of applications. It was recently reported that recruiters were receiving over 40,000 applications for fewer than 150 job vacancies.

As one employer, a senior HR director at a leading global investment bank, told me:

> This year we advertised 16 graduate jobs. From this we received 9,000 applications. Can you imagine what 9,000 applications looks like, or how long it takes to process them all? We used to say we respond to all applicants within 48 hours, but with 9,000 applications there's simply no chance. We're resigned to receiving lots of complaints.

Changing patterns of graduate vacancies

As a parent, you'll want to ensure that your child is planning to enter a graduate job with a future; not one that's on its way out. This section explores the changing nature of the graduate job market, plotting the recruitment patterns of leading graduate employers, and it details all the major employment sectors, showing what share of the graduate market employers in these sectors control.

If you want to help your child predict where demand for jobs in the future will be, take a look at the figure below. It looks at the distribution of graduate jobs across Britain's leading 100 or so graduate recruiters. It plots recruitment patterns over a period of four years (2007–11). Some very interesting patterns emerge ...

How graduate vacancies changed by sector or industry (2007–11)

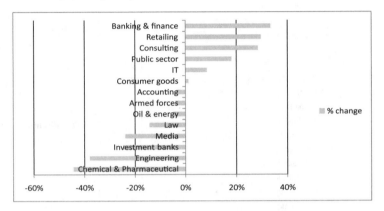

Source: High Fliers, 2011

Comparing graduate recruitment in 2011 with 2007 shows how, over a four-year period, the recession has impacted on the distribution of job vacancies. For jobs in chemicals and pharmaceuticals, the economic downturn has played havoc with recruitment plans, leading to a fall of almost 45% in job opportunities. Sectors such as engineering and investment banking have also been hard hit by the crunch: between 2007 and 2011, new jobs for graduates in engineering fell by a staggering 37.9%.

Not all industries and sectors, however, have suffered the same plight. Remember those pictures of newly unemployed city bankers carrying their cardboard boxes of office possessions? Well, pictures can be deceptive. During the period covered by the above graph, jobs in banking and finance have grown by an incredible 33.5% – up one-third on the previous period. Retailing has also seen a four-year increase in job opportunities, as has consulting.

Distribution of graduate job vacancies (2011)

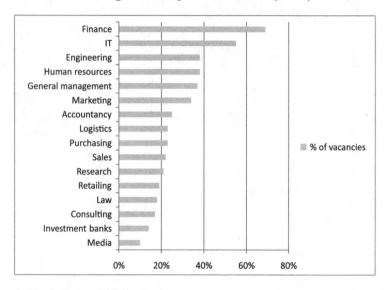

Source: High Fliers, 2011

The figure above shows job vacancies in 2011. Again, this emphasises the dominance of finance and IT. The strength of these sectors has not diminished, nor has it really changed for much of the past decade, despite the recession.

The same figure also shows that while engineering may have seen a fall in job vacancies in the past four years, it still remains the third largest sector for graduates.

The search for stability

Since the recession, jobs in the public sector, teaching, and social and welfare professions have all seen steep rises in numbers of applications. It seems that the recession has had a tempering effect on students' career aspirations, and jobs in the public sector acquire a new lustre.

It's as if graduates put on recession goggles: when the economy is strong, high-risk jobs become attractive; when the economy is weak, jobs offering security and stability, become more alluring.

According to researchers at the Higher Education Careers Service Unit (HECSU), post-recession the number of graduates beginning work as medical practitioners increased by 15%. The number of nurses and midwives has grown by 3%, while physiotherapists, occupational therapists, and speech therapists have seen their numbers increase by 17%.

Teaching has also become far more popular with new graduates. In recent years, the number of new secondary school teachers has risen by 14%. Jobs in educational administration have also proved popular, doubling in numbers in less than 12 months. Social work has also witnessed a post-recession boom, with recruits growing by 55%.

Task

Talk to your child about the impact of the economic market on their future career plans. To what extent are your child's career ambitions dependent on a buoyant job market? Are the jobs that they intend to pursue vulnerable or immune to economic downturn? If they are vulnerable – what's Plan B?

Who are the recruiters?

In 2011, High Fliers Research asked more than 16,000 final-year students at a range of UK universities the question 'Which employers do you think offer the best opportunities for graduates?' Between them, students named 800 different organisations. Of these, the most popular 100 were those listed below.

Look at this list. You'll see a range of organisations represented, from a broad spectrum of industries and sectors. In particular, note how many fall within the financial services sector. Despite the economic downturn, financial services remain the engine room of the UK graduate recruitment market.

Note also the multitude of retailers and law firms. Gone are the days when manufacturing and engineering firms headed up the graduate job market. Today, the job market is dominated by 'thin air' firms – organisations that trade on brands, expertise and knowledge.

Accenture	Cadbury	HSBC
Airbus	Cancer Research UK	IBM
Aldi	Centrica	Jaguar Land Rover
Allen & Overy	Citi	John Lewis
Arcadia Group	Civil Service	J.P. Morgan
Army	Clifford Chance	KPMG
Arup	Credit Suisse	L'Oréal
Asda	Deloitte	Lidl
AstraZeneca	Deutsche Bank	Linklaters
Atkins	Diageo	Lloyd's
BAE Systems	DLA Piper	Lloyds Banking Group
Bain & Company	E.ON	Local Government
Baker & McKenzie	EDF	Marks & Spencer
Balfour Beatty	Ernst & Young	Mars
Barclays Bank	ExxonMobil	McDonald's
Barclays Capital	Foreign Office	Restaurants
BBC	Freshfields Bruckhaus	McKinsey &
BDO Stoy Hayward	Deringer	Company
Bloomberg	GCHQ	Merrill Lynch
BNP Paribas	GlaxoSmithKline	MI5 – The Security
Boots Company	Goldman Sachs	Service
Boston Consulting	Google	Microsoft
Group	Grant Thornton	Ministry of Defence
BP	Herbert Smith	Morgan Stanley
BT	Hogan Lovells	Nestlé

Network Rail	RAF	Sony
NHS	RBS Group	Teach First
npower	Rolls-Royce	Tesco
Nuclear Graduates	Royal Navy	The Co-operative
Oxfam	Saatchi & Saatchi	Group
Penguin	Sainsbury's	Transport for
Police	Santander	London
Pricewaterhouse	Shell	UBS
Coopers	Siemens	Unilever
Procter & Gamble	Sky	Vodafone
QinetiQ	Slaughter and May	WPP

Task

Discuss these organisations with your child. Ask them to select a top 10 of preferred organisations. What type of employer appears in the list? What industries or sectors are represented – and which aren't? Are there any surprising omissions? Are any of these organisations unknown to you? To find out more about these organisations, what they do and the type of graduates they're looking to recruit, see www.highfliersresearch.com

---

Don't forget SMEs

One thing all the organisations in the list above have in common is size. All are officially large organisations, each employing well over 1,000 people. They're also well known, appearing in countless newspaper articles, TV advertisements, news programmes, and of course, university careers fairs. This means that when asked about which organisations they'd like to work for, many students select those which they're familiar with.

But it's important to realise that even though firms such as PricewaterhouseCoopers recruit up to 1,000 university leavers each year, and are instantly recognisable as graduate recruiters, such organisations represent only a tiny proportion of the overall graduate recruitment market. Most employers of UK graduates are unlikely to ever appear in any of the above lists. That's because they're small and medium-sized organisations or, as they're known to economists, SMEs.

> ❝ SMEs typically employ fewer than 200 people, although many are far smaller. In the UK, SMEs account for the vast majority of organisations and as such, for graduates, represent a huge and often untapped employment opportunity. ❞

Not that you'd know it. Graduate recruitment fairs and other careers events remain dominated by large, well-known 'brand' employers. It's not surprising then that so many students should remain fixated on the big firms because often it's all they have to go on.

Fortunately, in recent years, university careers services have begun to build up their SME contacts. No longer are recruitment activities and events reserved solely for large organisations. Nevertheless, when discussing possible employers with your child, remember that not all graduate recruiters are household names. In fact, you've probably never heard of most of them.

Task

Talk to your child about the type of company they want to work for: have they set their sights on a top 100 graduate recruiter? Ensure they don't dismiss smaller companies where there is both opportunity and potential to grow.

4
Make your child employable

You may have heard the word 'employability' used as a buzz word, a trendy phrase batted around by journalists and academics. As this chapter shows, it's far more important. It's nothing less than the key to 21st century job markets. In this chapter we explore the meaning of employability and identify the top four employability skills that all employers, regardless of who they're looking to hire, demand from graduates.

Despite the mountains of literature surrounding it, there are really only two things you need to know about 'employability'. First, it means much more than just being employed. The words might sound the same but, believe me, they're not. Between them spans a world of difference.

> **Employability is to employment what being wildly attractive to the opposite sex is to being married. One opens up a world of endless possibilities; the other, by restricting you to just one option, closes them down.**

And don't think that as long as you've got a job, you're automatically *employable*. Sure, you might once have been, but the chances are you'll only find out whether you are still employable if, for whatever reason, you have to go looking for another job. That's why, upon losing their jobs, many people in recent years have been disappointed to discover that they possess very little employability.

People who are truly employable who lose their jobs have usually, by lunchtime, gone on to find better paying jobs with rival competitors. That's employability – being able to find a better or equal-paying job when you really need it.

The second thing you need to know about employability is that it's not entirely in your own hands. In fact, it's all to do with the theory of relativity. Think of it like this:

> **Imagine your child goes for a job interview. Based on the job description, he possesses all the right qualifications, skills, work experience, motivation, confidence and drive. Success should be a foregone conclusion. Shouldn't it?**

Not necessarily. Because employability isn't simply an *absolute* – something you either possess or don't possess. It's also relative. In other words, it's all to do with how well you compare against the opposition.

When applying for jobs, your child will be competing against other graduates from almost identical backgrounds, social and educational. Success or failure at interview will depend not only on how well your child performs during selection but also on how they compare relative to the opposition. And you thought the theory of relativity was just about time travel.

What does employability mean?

There are no set definitions of employability despite the fact that you'll see it used frequently in the press.

Possibly the best known definition used by many universities is the one developed by the higher education think tank ESECT (Enhancing Student Employability Co-ordination Team):

> ❝ Employability is a set of achievements – skills, understandings and personal attributes – that make graduates more likely to gain employment and be successful in their chosen occupations. ❞

As definitions go, this is probably as good as it gets. Employability – being employable – requires:

- skill, and an understanding of the job market and the world of work
- personal attributes, such as personality, motivation, sense of humour, contacts
- and of course, credentials such as academic qualifications.

All these skills and attributes, in a nutshell, are what your child will need to acquire in order to be employable.

Although the idea of employability is just catching on in universities, in the job market, employers have been conversant with the idea of employability for some time.

> **In a survey of 500 recruitment managers, 64%** said that when hiring graduates, employability skills were more important to their firm than any specific occupational, technical or academic knowledge gained from the graduate's degree. **"**

In other words, for the majority of graduate recruiters, what makes a graduate stand out from the competition isn't the degree they've studied but the other ingredients that 'employable' graduates bring to organisations. Ingredients such as: skills, attitude, energy, insight, potential for development, and the ever-valuable willingness to make a good cup of tea.

What few employers really care about, it seems, is the subject of the degree. Many students and parents find this hard to take in, but it's true.

In Part 2 you'll find more information on choosing a degree, and in Part 3 we go into detail to help you understand the skills your child will need, and how to go about getting them.

Task

Talk to your child about the concept of employability. Is it a word they're familiar with? What do they think employability means and what do they think it takes to be not just employed but employable? Try to use examples from your own career.

5

The future of your child's career

Good career decisions require an understanding of not only yourself and the opportunities available to you, but they also call in no small measure for the ability to make informed decisions about the future.

O f course, predicting the future is anything but an exact science. However, as you are about to find out, our predictions about the future are often surprisingly accurate. The trouble is, if these predictions don't fit with what people want to hear, it's remarkably easy to dismiss them. After all, they're only guesswork, right?

Wrong. Predictions are fundamentally different from guesses. Guesses are based on wishful thinking and hope; predictions are based on a careful reading of past trends, current data and scientific modelling.

In today's overheated job market, the ability to make informed predictions about the future is even more important, particularly given the costs of going to university.

> ❝ Choose the wrong subject combination or opt for the wrong vocational degree course and your child could easily find himself, in future years, packing a CV full of redundant skills and obsolete qualifications. ❞

Back to the future

As a parent, making predictions will be second nature to you. Since your child was born, you have been making predictions about their future – trying to see around corners, doing your best to make sure that your child is well equipped for the years ahead.

Because this book is about helping you to help your child find a job after university, it's important that part of it should include trying to decipher what the future job market, future economy, even the future world might look like in the years ahead. Only by acquiring an informed understanding of some of the major trends and developments that are set to impact over the next few years can sound career decisions be made.

To help you and your child make your own career predictions, this chapter provides a selection of some of the key trends which, according to experts, will impact on the future job market.

 To be employable tomorrow, preparation has to begin today. 〞

Below are a range of key predictions which, if accurate, are likely to have a significant impact on your child's life and career.

If some of these predications appear far-fetched, consider this . . .

After completing university, your son or daughter is likely to be working for around half a century. For a 21-year-old student who graduates in 2012, retirement will be in approximately 2062.

Now, travel back in time from 2012 by a similar number of years. You arrive at 1962. Think of the changes that have occurred since 1962 in technology, in the global economy, in communications, in popular culture, in politics, in the status of women, in the world itself.

If only a small proportion of the changes that have occurred between 1962 and today take place during the next 50 years, we can still expect the world of the 2060s to be radically different from today.

Suddenly, the predictions which follow may no longer appear quite so futuristic.

Society

Globalisation 3.0

Globalisation is often spoken about as if it is a new concept. It isn't. Globalisation of trade, products, markets and even ideas has been occurring for centuries. Globalisation 2.0 took this a step further, harnessing information technology and the internet to create a much more global marketplace. Next up is Globalisation 3.0 – a fully-connected, interdependent way of doing business.

In Globalisation 3.0 we are about to encounter an era of almost total exposure to people, products and ideas from everywhere, all the time. As Richard Watson writes in *Future Files: A brief history of the next 50 years* (Nicholas Brealey, 2009):

> ❝ Everything from countries and computers to gadgets and global banking will be hyperlinked together. ❞

Thanks in no small part to technology, your child will be living and working in an era when globalisation will be revolutionising how people work, when they work and even where they work.

Globalisation 3.0 will be all about using computer technology to open up global opportunities. Even jobs that are all about the provision of local services will source products, ideas, information and advice from people and organisations all over the world. In Globalisation 2.0, jobs were outsourced from the developed to the developing world. In Globalisation 3.0 it will be far easier to work on projects and initiatives with co-workers located around the planet.

The implications of Globalisation 3.0 are mind-boggling. One billion people are currently online and this number is set to double within a decade or so. There are also 2.5 billion talking to each other via mobile phones. With this come benefits and risks. In exchange for immediate information and access, concerns will be raised about online security and appropriate levels of data access.

Globalisation 3.0 will bring the world's economies closer than ever before. This will also apply to the world's workers. Jobs will go to whoever has the best skills and education – no matter where they're located.

In pursuit of 'graduate' jobs, skilled workers will travel across borders, either physically or virtually. Loyalty to organisations will dwindle. To accomplish tasks, expert teams will come together, complete a project and then disband. And because they're based around the world, in different time zones, you might never even get to meet your co-workers.

Jobs to think about

- Linguists, particularly those skilled in Mandarin, Cantonese and Russian
- Market research experts
- Cultural translators
- Chief information officers
- 'Cloud' IT experts.

Ageing society

As the baby boomer generation gets older new job opportunities are opening up. Currently, there are over 20 million adults in the UK aged 50-plus. In Japan, the situation is even more advanced. Between 2005 and 2015, the percentage of the population aged over 75 is forecast to increase by 36% per year – a population shift which will place intense strain on the country's tax levy, which will have to grow by 175% simply to cover costs associated with an ageing population.

Compared to other generations these UK baby boomers are wealthy, holding on to around 80% of all the country's wealth. They are also time-wealthy, spending twice as much on leisure and entertainment as the under-30s, and generating up to 40% of UK consumer spending (a figure worth around £260 billion per annum). And don't expect them to slow down: this generation expect to continue enjoying their current quality of life and have no plans to reduce their aspirations.

The trouble is no one yet seems to have told today's manufacturers, retailers, entertainment providers and designers, who press on in their futile quest of only making things for younger people.

66 For some entrepreneurs, this blind spot will be a source of huge profit: any service, organisation or product that can meet the needs of Britain's ageing population will be at a major advantage. 99

Jobs to think about

- Anything related to pharmaceuticals
- Wellbeing
- Medical tourism
- Healthcare planning
- Designer-tourism
- Age-friendly technology

Go East

As the 21st century progresses, centres of world economic, political and military power are forecast to shift eastwards as new and more powerful economies overtake those in the West. Consumer spending in China is expected to hit over $2.2trillion soon and, between them, Kuwait, Saudi Arabia, UAE, Bahrain, Qatar and Oman have over $1trillion invested in capital projects which analysts expect to double or even triple in the coming decades.

Jobs to think about

- Linguists (Mandarin, Russian, Arabic)
- Cultural translators
- Currency dealers
- Financial investors

Attitudes to debt

As we have seen, these are already difficult times for your child's generation (known to sociologists as Generation Y). The bad news is the future looks no less challenging. Over the next decade, growing numbers of students will be graduating from university with up to £50,000 of debts.

So far, few seem to have realised some of the wider social and economic implications tied up in having large numbers of educated, ambitious, socially mobile and, for the country, key individuals tied up with so much debt that they're unable to get on with their lives.

But once the penny has dropped, expect to see a raft of financial changes. With people living longer, look out for the first 50-year mortgage. Family mortgages will also become more common as attitudes to lifelong debt change.

Unlike previous generations, Generation Y is unlikely to inherit much money from parents. It's not that baby boomers don't have assets or are unwilling to share them, it's simply because most of these assets will be used up in supporting Generation Y in its decade-long quest for home ownership.

Jobs to think about

- Creative mortgage planners
- Financial-literacy planners
- Money coaches
- Private landlords
- Space consultants (i.e. people who help maximise the value of business spaces)

The environment and the three Rs

Ongoing concerns over the environment will only accelerate as the century progresses, along with the mantra of the new three Rs – Reuse, Recycle and Reduce.

Sustainability will be a major issue with governments and organisations competing with one another to demonstrate their super-green credentials. At the same time, worries about energy shortage and what happens post-fossil fuels will spark a major raft of global investment, with significant impact on the job market.

Jobs to think about

- Environmental impact assessors
- Alternative energy scientists
- Sustainability consultants
- Environmental advisers
- Environmental lawyers

Technology

GRIN and bear it

Machines are destined to play a major role in the future: computers will eventually overtake humans in the intelligence stakes. GRIN (Genetics;

Robotics; Internet and Nanotechnology) will transform how we live, work and experience the world around us, while at the same time, contemporary machines such as personal computers will be replaced by ever more sophisticated personal, hand-held devices.

IT departments will be a thing of the past, taking with them legions of computer technicians and IT managers. Rapid advances in 'Cloud' IT storage facilities will mean that rooms packed with servers will be redundant.

Jobs to think about

- Jobs connected to Genetics, Robotics, Internet and Nanotechnology (GRIN)
- Cloud technologists

Digital nomads

Advances in technology will make it easier for employers to recruit using online recruitment and selection methods. Technology will also mean the end of commuting to work as more people opt to work from home.

But there is a downside. Better technology will blend the space between 'work' and 'home', meaning that increasingly people will be expected to be available for work even when, nominally, on holiday. Not that this term will mean much. Concepts such as 'holidays' were invented during the industrial revolution and, in a post-industrial landscape, will rapidly become meaningless.

Jobs to think about

- Stress consultants
- Digital designers
- HR consultants
- Surveillance experts

The workplace

Big firms go bust

In 1917, Forbes published a list of the world's leading 100 firms. Today, a century later, just 13 of these organisations still exist as independent entities. The rest have either gone out of business or been subsumed by other companies.

This is entirely predictable. Studies show that most large organisations last less than 100 years. No matter how big they are, or how wealthy, most of today's big companies can expect to go the same way. Call it evolution, call it Darwinism at work. Never forget the old saying: how do you buy a small company? Buy a big one and wait.

Jobs to think about

- Professional agents (people you pay to manage your career for you)
- Small business entrepreneurs
- Outsourcing experts
- Workplace consultants

Digital Taylorism

Frederick Taylor (1856–1915) was an American mechanical engineer who had a serious thing about *efficiency*. In fact, he was obsessed with it, spending much of his career searching for the 'one best way' to accomplish industrial processes. Taylor's ideas on 'scientific' management, quality and time-and-motion studies became highly influential throughout the 20th century, redesigning factory work, particularly in heavy engineering fields like car production.

From the 1930s onwards, Taylor's talent for applying scientific approaches to the workplace helped transform industrial processes throughout the world. Frederick Taylor was never mentioned in dispatches during the Second World War, but as tanks rolled off American and British production lines, his ideas proved how efficiency and planning could make a serious difference.

Since then, Taylor's ideas have been applied to everything from fast food to digital cameras and MP3 players. But in the future, a new evolution of Taylorism is set to redesign the workplace: *Digital Taylorism*.

Digital Taylorism is set to do to the world of white-collar workers what a century ago it did to the world of the blue-collar worker. Until now, 'knowledge workers' have enjoyed large amounts of autonomy; that will soon come to an end. New technology will enable employers to capture key information about how knowledge-worker jobs are carried out. Once this knowledge has been sorted, codified and repacked, it can be outsourced to wherever is cheapest in the world.

> **❝ Work that was once deemed highly skilled will be accessible, demystified and reproducible – in effect, up for grabs to the lowest bidder. ❞**

Digital Taylorism will cause havoc in professional jobs such as the legal profession, accountancy, academia, publishing, architecture, medicine, design and IT. Any industry that was once considered 'high-end' in terms of knowledge and expertise is in for a rude awakening, as are any jobs that once charged a premium for helping non-specialists decipher and decode complex information. Over the next decade, the beneficiaries of this new and accessible knowledge will be the fast growing economies of Brazil, Russia, India and China – economies that are well placed to offer organisations an abundance of people with high skills and low-wage expectations.

Jobs to think about

Those that can't easily be outsourced overseas and require the following skills:

- Artistic
- Design
- Specialist craft

Knowledge society downfall

Since the economic downturn, the world of work has become more, rather than less, aligned to graduate entry jobs. The reason for this can be summed up in two words: Knowledge Society.

For the past two decades, the idea of the Knowledge Society has been highly influential, particularly in Western economies. Underpinning this idea is a belief that in the future 'knowledge' will be a key commodity, which will be bought and sold around the world.

In the 19th century, iron and steel were the most valuable economic commodities. In the 20th it was knowledge. As we have seen, however, digital Taylorism changes all that. Once knowledge has been captured and codified, it's easily reproduced, replicated and repackaged, and once this happens its value plummets.

Another problem with the idea of the Knowledge Society is that it overlooks the impact that is being made by computers and IT. In the years ahead, computers will be doing more.

> ❝ Computers will do most of the remembering and thinking for us, and automate most of the work that comprises the knowledge economy. We will still want to learn the knowledge and skills; they just won't be as commercially valuable as they are today.

Robots and machine tools have already done this to some physical jobs such as skilled factory work, and future robots will continue to automate many other jobs, even surgery and construction. 〞

Ian Pearson, futurologist

This means that for much of the next 50 years the market value of knowledge will be reduced. True, for their expertise and insights, some highly sought-after knowledge workers will continue to draw huge salaries; but as a proportion of the overall workforce, such people will be in the minority.

In purely economic terms, the developing world's investment in education and technology will produce a 'leapfrog' effect, as both China and India overtake the West, offering a unique blend of high-level skills at bargain basement costs. Already, China has more students at university than the United States, and India isn't far behind. At the same time, overseas students are dominating European and US postgraduate programmes – particularly in science and engineering.

❝ By the time today's school-starters leave university, the knowledge economy will be history. The economically useful skills will be those the kids learned in the playground, on the school bus and the night club. Just as the CEO spends a lot of time on golf courses and dinners with clients, so most people will focus on interaction face to face with other people. 〞

Ian Pearson, futurologist

But it's not all bad news, for replacing the knowledge society will be its successor, the Care Society.

The care society

One thing robots and computers are never going to be good at is dealing one-on-one with people. As physical and intellectual tasks are delegated increasingly to smart machines, what Ian Pearson refers to as 'those softer bits of our jobs', e.g. human interaction, are set to grow.

> ❝ Sometimes this will be in roles such as caring, sales and marketing, entertaining, or providing personal services such as therapy, counselling, training and so on. Sometimes it will just be spending time with people. This might not sound much of a job, but as the economic focus shifts from GDP to quality of life measures, we will value other aspects of wellbeing above material provision, which in any case will continue to fall in relative price into the far future. ❞

Ian Pearson, futurologist

As the population ages and more people migrate to online communities and neighbourhoods, the value of personal contact, personal consultation, personal attention and person-centred expertise will increase. This in turn will lead to a rapid growth of care-orientated jobs and professions – jobs which offer the types of services and functions that people used to receive from families, the state and local communities. These jobs will mix sophisticated IT communications with individual contact – a unique 21st century blend of the old and new.

Jobs to think about

- Nurses
- Carers
- Personal trainers

- Lifestyle consultants
- Dieticians
- Online counsellors
- Digital therapists
- Neighbourhood consultants (people whose role it is to help fragmented neighbourhoods communicate and liaise more effectively)
- Social workers
- Community mentors
- Teachers

Youth job markets set to return

For the past 20 years, jobs for non-graduate young people have been disappearing as employers, surrounded by a surfeit of graduate talent, have come to regard a degree as the minimum entry standard. But as demographic changes, combined with an ageing population accelerate, demand for young workers will accelerate. As a result, new jobs will appear designed specifically for young, non-graduate workers. Some of these will be organised along the lines of formal apprenticeships. Others, however, will be more flexible, fitting around the availability of the young person and run in conjunction with local education providers.

This isn't to say there won't be graduate jobs. There will, but at the same time governments in the West will invest more resources in developing jobs for those who in the current job market are excluded from work opportunities. Currently, the gap between graduate jobs and those for unskilled workers is wider than ever, with serious implications for social cohesion. In the next few years, you can expect more government-led initiatives to help bridge the gap.

Handy work returns

As digital Taylorism turns office life into a highly organised, semi-industrial, factory experience, the popularity of craft-level jobs such as carpentry, plumbing, electrician, potting, gardening, metal working, painting, car maintenance will return with a vengeance, only in future these jobs will be undertaken increasingly by university graduates and other ex-knowledge workers.

The rediscovery of manual and craft work will be a major feature of the mid-21st century as, gradually, 20th century definitions of 'white-collar' and 'blue-collar' work become insignificant. Not that these jobs will be entirely retrospective-looking: the craft workers of the 21st century will, through virtual internet technology, operate on a global basis, meeting the needs of customers and organisations around the world.

Jobs to think about

- Carpentry and joinery
- Designer jewellery
- Bespoke tailoring
- Fashion design
- Pet grooming
- Garden consultancy and design

Education

Degrees plus

By the next decade, being a student will become the most populated occupation in the world. In turn, as more people leave university with degrees and postgraduate qualifications, being able to offer prospective employers more than simply a piece of paper will become ever more important. Here are some of the ways that the face of further education is set to change.

- Universities across the world will redesign their curricula to include work-based placements and work-related learning.

- Academics will be recruited almost exclusively from industry and universities will be judged solely on their destination statistics – information on the number of graduates to find graduate employment, and in what sector.

- Changes in funding will result in more courses being offered in STEM subjects (science, technology, engineering and mathematics).

- In some universities, arts and humanities faculties will close. As a result, graduates with degrees in these subjects will become highly sought-after, as employers look to recruit them for their creative thinking.

Task

What are your own predictions for the next 50 years? How will life, work, politics, culture and technology change? What will be the impact of these changes on your child? How well prepared would you say they were for the challenges of the future?

Part 2

Planning for university

Part 2 looks at the question of university. The cost of going to uni has rocketed in recent years, but is it still a good investment? If you are helping your child through uni, which you probably are, will you ever see a return on your money? And what degree should your child study?

We'll also help you find out the crucial questions you and your child should be asking unis before applying. Unis now need to answer questions about their graduate's employability, and you need to start asking them.

6

What's the point of a degree?

Given the changes taking place in the job market, asking what's the point of going to university is as reasonable question as any to start with. After all, as a parent, this will be a decision that you and your child will need to take – a decision with serious financial and career-related consequences.

ver the past decade, in the UK alone, the number of students going to university has doubled. At the same time, to meet the demand, universities have been expanding rapidly. So far, that demand seems a long way off from reducing.

At the time of writing, more students than ever are competing for university places, particularly those offering the most prestigious courses. Not that university is the only option in town. In recent years, apprenticeships have become increasingly popular, particularly in sectors such as engineering and manufacturing. Some have claimed that the new popularity of vocational alternatives to higher education herald an end to the golden era of university – an era when numbers of graduates increased tenfold – not just in the UK, but around the world.

Global vision

- Worldwide, 63 million people are currently enrolled in higher education. Being a student is now the world's most populated 'occupation'.
- China has more students enrolled at university than the USA.
- Asia produces more scientists and engineers than Europe and the USA combined.
- In the US, half of all PhDs in engineering, mathematics and computer science are from overseas.
- In the UK, less than half of students on science-based postgraduate courses are British.

Source: 'Education, globalisation and the future of the knowledge economy', European Educational Research Journal, Ashton, D., Brown, P., Lauder, H. (2008)

But is the university bubble about to burst, or is going to university still the solid gold career ticket that it has always been?

Essential for certain subjects

If your child wants the type of job associated with graduates, as we have seen in chapter 2, having a degree isn't an option: it's mandatory. Opticians, doctors, solicitors, teachers, dentists, architects, computer programmers, human resources managers, journalists, fashion designers, pharmacists, engineers, software developers, car designers, social workers, surveyors, lecturers, researchers and nurses are all increasingly graduate-only occupations. If your child is interested in exploring one of these jobs, going to university is an all-but given.

A degree is for life . . .

Jobs for graduates also, on the whole, offer greater lifelong financial benefits. It is important to stress 'lifelong'. In today's crunched job markets, financial rewards – even for graduates – can take a number of years to realise. Rather than having a short-term advantage, the economic benefits of most university degree courses accrue over time.

> 66 According to a study of 2005 graduates, within just three years after graduating from university, more than eight out of 10 graduates were working in jobs defined by the government as 'graduate occupations'. 99

What do graduates think?

Compared to other workers, graduates are more likely to register high levels of job satisfaction. In one survey, almost nine out of 10 said they were either 'very satisfied' or 'fairly satisfied' with their career to date.

Another study conducted by researchers from the University of Warwick explored career outcomes three years after graduation by following up those who graduated from higher education in 1999. A similar pattern emerged. Graduates were enthusiastic about the advantages of having a degree and claimed that the experience of going to university gave them numerous career-related advantages. Not only were they better at writing, analysis, problem-solving and presentation skills, they were also able to apply these skills in their job roles.

According to the *Student Experience Report 2007* from UNITE, 94% of the 1,600-plus students surveyed reported that 'going to university is a worthwhile investment and a natural progression from school'.

What employers really think of graduates

If you want to know whether going to university is a good career move for your child, you can't do better than talk to a panel of employers. After all, they're the people who ultimately make the hiring decisions. So what do they see in graduates?

Evidence exists to suggest that even with rising numbers of graduates entering the market demand for degree holders shows no sign of having reached saturation. In fact, employers are increasing rather than decreasing their graduate recruitment targets.

Writing about the value of a university degree, Terence Perrin, chairman of the Association of Graduate Recruiters (AGR), the largest body of graduate recruiters in the UK, said:

> There is no doubt that a university degree still has a very high currency with employers and a profound effect on a person's earning potential over a lifetime. Our membership of over 800 organisations involved in graduate recruitment still attaches great

value to a university education and has remained committed to recruiting graduate talent through the recession. A degree remains an extremely worthwhile investment. **99**

Task

Talk to your child about their reasons for wanting to go to university. Try to highlight the top three reasons for enrolment. Where does employability come? What do your child's priorities mean for the next few years? Are your child's reasons and rankings the same as yours?

7
Does it matter what you study?

'Frame it and forget it!' So began one recruitment manager's welcoming address to new graduates. It wasn't that the manager had a problem with degrees – his firm remains one of the biggest recruiters of graduates in the UK. The point he was making was simply that in today's workplace the majority of graduates are recruited for their personal and transferable skills, not their subject knowledge. This may be a harsh message to have to take in on your first day at work, but it seems that when it comes to landing a top job the actual degree subject is now far less important than most people think.

To help your child make informed decisions about which subject to choose at university, this chapter looks at what graduates from different subject clusters do after six months of graduation. Again, this data relates specifically to first-degree subjects and was collected by careers services shortly after graduation.

Any degree will do . . . or will it?

Every year, around two-thirds of jobs advertised for degree-holders are open to applicants from any academic degree subject. If anything, the proportion is growing. Such jobs cover a broad range of industries and professions, particularly those involving people-based services.

In human resources, for example, 95% of all graduate vacancies are open to applicants from any degree background. Similarly high percentages have also been reported in retail management (86% 'any' subject), advertising and marketing (78%) and business administration (63%).

Even in the tightly regulated world of finance, more jobs are opening up to non-specialists. In fact, 78% of jobs in accountancy and banking are non-subject specific, with firms like Bank of America, Deloitte, Ernst & Young and Lloyds TSB accepting applications from students with both vocational and non-vocational subjects.

But by far the most radical shift has taken place in the computing sector. Historically, jobs in IT have tended to target those with technical qualifications. Not any more. Since the late 1990s the global downturn in IT has prompted many firms to re-think their recruitment strategies. A focus on teamwork, customer needs and staff development has emerged, along with a drive to broaden the talent base.

66 Currently, around six out of every 10 jobs advertised in IT are open to graduates from any subject, transforming the sector into one of the largest graduate recruiters in the UK. Bill Gates was right when he warned: 'Be nice to nerds, chances are you'll end up working for one.' If you're a student at university today, at this rate you probably will. 99

A recent national graduate destination survey showed how much the subject of a degree does *not* relate to the graduate job secured.

Take psychology for example. On leaving university, graduates from this subject are five times more likely to work in a bank or building society than go into clinical psychology (not that you'd suspect it from watching psychological dramas like *Cracker*). The same principle applies to other popular and not so popular subjects. Despite enjoying some of the highest employment levels in the UK, six months after leaving university, graduates from media studies are more likely to work behind a counter than behind a camera or on a magazine. What can you do with a degree in geography? Well, just about anything it seems, except jobs involving applied geography.

Not even scientists are immune to this phenomenon. Graduates with physics degrees have more chance of working in business and finance than doing anything remotely scientific.

Understandably, students and their parents are often surprised at just how flexible the job market for graduates has become, and the number of firms that are dropping the requirement for specific subjects. Learning that not all barristers have law degrees or accountants have accountancy degrees can be both liberating and perplexing. As one graduate challenged me recently, 'So what *can* I do with a degree in American history?'

My answer, essentially, was that it was up to her. What the majority of graduates go on to do after leaving university is shaped not by their choice of degree subject but by their level of 'employability' – their own unique combination of skills, attitudes and work experience.

> 66 As a certain US president might have said: ask not what you can do with a degree in American history. Ask what a degree in American history can do for you. 99

For many students and parents, realising that a degree isn't enough to confer lifelong employability comes as a shock. But it shouldn't. For years, employers have been growing more ambivalent about which degree subjects they prefer. As higher education has grown, the range of courses and qualifications on offer has spiralled incredibly. Most HR managers simply can't keep up with the huge diversity of degree subjects and combinations on offer. Now, when it comes to writing job advertisements, few recruiters can be bothered to specify specific subject disciplines. All most write is:

> 66 Preferred degree subject: any. 99

So, while there are exceptions, as far as most recruiters are concerned, having a degree is a given, virtually taken for granted. What counts, and what marks the difference between getting a job and not, is your child's employability skills (see Part 3).

Having said that, when it comes to getting a job, some degree subjects produce more impressive employment statistics than others. This might seem contradictory – after all, haven't we just been saying that in the competition for jobs, degree subjects aren't as important as you might think?

Yes. But that doesn't mean to say that some degree subjects don't produce better employment statistics than others. As a parent, it's essential that you know which these subjects are.

Degrees with the best (and worst) employability track records

Arts, creative arts and humanities

Forget what you might have read in the media about 'useless' arts degrees. Studies show that six months after graduation, in comparison with the overall graduate employment rate, graduates from art and design, media studies and performing arts achieve higher-than-average levels of employment. This might surprise you, as traditionally media studies and the like has been thought of as a 'soft' or easier degree subject.

Where employment rates tend to be lower are in subjects such as English, history and languages. But this has to be interpreted carefully. From these subjects, many graduates have traditionally enrolled for postgraduate training, including teacher training. This has a depressive impact on their overall levels of employment.

Destinations of first degree arts, creative arts and humanities graduates, six months after graduation

	Total Number	Entering employment	Entering further study/training	Working and studying	Unemployed at time of survey	Other
Art and design	12,570	64.6%	7.0%	5.2%	12.2%	11.0%
English	8,620	56.3%	21.4%	8.0%	7.9%	9.2%
History	8,135	51.7%	21.8%	7.0%	9.8%	9.7%
Media studies	4,340	67.5%	6.5%	3.7%	12.3%	10.0%
Modern languages	6,620	55.3%	20.5%	6.7%	8.5%	9.0%
Performing arts	7,635	62.4%	14.5%	7.5%	7.9%	7.7%
All subjects	220,065	61.4%	14.1%	8.1%	7.9%	8.5%

Source: HECSU 2010

Biomedical subjects

Biomedical subjects have traditionally attracted high levels of employment and compared to other job sectors, demand in this field is the nearest you can get to being recession-proof. Also, degree courses in biomedical subjects are highly vocational and while studying, graduates tend to acquire high-value work experience. All this, as you can see in the table below, makes a substantial difference in the job market.

The table illustrates how well over 80% of graduates in medicine, nursing, physiotherapy and occupational therapy had secured employment within just six months after graduation. This was significantly higher than the UK all-subject average, which at the time of the survey stood at just 61.4%.

Destinations of biomedical graduates, six months after graduation

	Total No.	Entering employment	Entering further study/ training	Working and studying	Unemployed at time of survey	Other
Anatomy, physiology and pathology	2,990	68.8%	16.1%	4.4%	5.6%	5.1%
Nursing	9,195	85.5%	1.4%	7.5%	1.7%	3.9%
Medicine	5,845	88.0%	5.3%	4.5%	0.2%	2.0%
Occupational therapy	1,240	86.2%	0.3%	2.5%	6.7%	4.3%
Physiotherapy	1,695	85.2%	1.8%	3.1%	5.7%	4.1%
Pharmacology, toxicology and pharmacy	1,910	64.8%	12.8%	15.7%	3.5%	3.1%
All subjects	220,065	61.4%	14.1%	8.1%	7.9%	8.5%

Source: HECSU 2010

Business and administrative studies

Over the past decade, business degrees have proved to be highly popular. Even at the height of the recession an additional 5,000 people applied to universities to study these courses. So is business a good investment?

On the whole, yes. Although the sector has been hit disproportionately hard by the economic downturn, business graduates remain highly employable. If levels of unemployment are above average, this is likely to be because compared to other subjects fewer students from these subjects opt to remain at university to enrol for higher degrees. Business graduates, on the whole, want to work after graduation; remaining in education is not uppermost in their career plans.

The table below presents the career destinations of business graduates from 2008. Don't be confused by the lower number of accountancy students entering employment. Look at the proportions who are engaged in 'working and studying'. If you want to become a professional accountant, a degree is only the first part of the training: next you need to secure a training contract with a firm of accountants, hence the 24.4% who at the time of the survey were doing just that.

Destinations of first degree business and administrative studies graduates from 2008, six months after graduation

	Total Number	Entering employment	Entering further study/ training	Working and studying	Unemployed at time of survey	Other
Accountancy	3,080	48.7%	7.8%	24.4%	10.9%	8.2%
Business and management	13,545	65.4%	7.5%	8.2%	8.9%	10.0%
Marketing	2,330	70.3%	5.0%	4.3%	9.6%	10.9%
All subjects	220,065	61.4%	14.1%	8.1%	7.9%	8.5%

Source: HECSU 2010

Engineering and building management

According to data, levels of employment amongst engineering and building management graduates remain buoyant, even given the detrimental impact the recession has had on the UK's building industry.

In the past, graduates from these subjects have been in great demand both nationally and internationally. In recent years, job markets, even for those with such specialist skills, have tightened. Evidence for this can be seen in the unemployment figures. During the past few years, as around the country building contracts have been torn up, all four subjects in this group have seen levels of unemployment rise steeply – and none more so than in architecture.

Despite the downturn, degrees in this cluster still registered above-average levels of employment, suggesting that once the economy has fully recovered normal business will be resumed.

Destinations of engineering and building graduates from 2008, six months after graduation

	Total Number	Entering employment	Entering further study/training	Working and studying	Unemployed at time of survey	Other
Architecture and building	5,360	62.2%	10.2%	11.2%	8.5%	6.8%
Civil engineering	1,730	69.4%	7.7%	8.9%	7.0%	4.6%
Electrical and electronic engineering	2,330	66.5%	9.6%	6.0%	11.0%	6.7%
Mechanical engineering	2,200	64.8%	11.7%	6.9%	10.1%	7.1%
All subjects	220,065	61.4%	14.1%	8.1%	7.9%	8.5%

Source: HESA DLHE 2007/08

Mathematics, IT and computing

“ Maths graduates are the graduate job market's equivalent of hens' teeth. Yes, they're that rare. **”**

Few subjects in recent years have been in so much demand as mathematics. Not that maths graduates have it all their own way. Employers' biggest criticism of maths graduates is that they can be weak on interpersonal skills. This can make them difficult citizens to shoehorn into teams, particularly those in which they will encounter non-mathematicians.

Maths graduates who realise this and who do their utmost to major on 'soft' skills, can find themselves in serious demand. Effective communication, team-working and decision-making are all skills which employers value as much as mathematical expertise. It will also help graduates market themselves effectively when applying for jobs.

Similar advice applies to computer science graduates. For these graduates, levels of employment have been fluctuating in recent years. Despite this, computer science graduates remain sought after. Employers appreciate that in an increasingly competitive market IT will remain a vital tool for commercial success. Graduates from this subject appear to realise this, for while there has been a slight fall-off in employment, more of them are enrolling for further and higher study.

Destinations of maths and IT graduates from 2008, six months after graduation

	Numbers graduating (survey respondents)	Entering employment	Entering further study/ training	Working and studying	Unemployed at time of survey	Other
Mathematics	3,645	46.4%	22.7%	13.8%	8.7%	8.5%
IT and Computing	9,450	63.6%	9.8%	4.6%	13.7%	8.3%
All subjects	220,065	61.4%	14.1%	8.1%	7.9%	8.5%

Source: HESA DLHE 2007/08

Science

One of the subject-clusters to have benefited from the changes to higher education funding arrangements appears to have been science.

Over the past few years, the number of students applying to study science at university has increased by over 10% per annum. According to figures published by UCAS, the total number of acceptances for physics degree courses saw an above average year-on-year rise of 12.9%. Applications for biology degrees rose by 10.2% in 2008. Similar increases were recorded in sports science (9.7%); physical geography (10.2%) and chemistry (4.1%).

This is good news because when it comes to science graduates, employers can't get enough of them.

According to the Confederation of British Industry (CBI), as the workplace becomes increasingly specialised, demand for science graduates will continue to rise. This prediction is backed up by employment projections prepared by the Council for Industry and Higher Education (CIHE). According to researchers, employer demand for graduates from science, technology, engineering and mathematics (STEM) subjects is set to grow significantly faster than that for all other degree subjects.

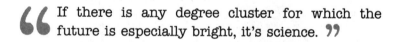 If there is any degree cluster for which the future is especially bright, it's science. ??

Destinations of first degree science graduates, six months after graduation

	Numbers graduating (survey respondents)	Entering employment	Entering further study/ training	Working and studying	Unemployed at time of survey	Other
Biology	3,495	51.1%	24.3%	6.9%	9.2%	8.5%
Chemistry	2,055	44.0%	34.5%	6.0%	8.5%	7.0%
Environmental, physical geographical and terrestrial sciences	2,545	54.5%	20.4%	6.4%	8.6%	10.1%
Physics	1,650	37.9%	36.3%	8.5%	9.1%	8.2%
Sports science	5,665	61.2%	16.6%	8.0%	5.6%	8.6%
All subjects	220,065	61.4%	14.1%	8.1%	7.9%	8.5%

Source: HESA DLHE 2010

Social sciences

Traditionally, in the months directly after leaving university, graduates from social science subjects have taken longer to settle into careers. This has led to their producing slightly lower than average levels of employment.

Added to this, social science graduates are more likely to remain in higher education for postgraduate study, including teacher training. Careers such as law, teaching, social work, counselling, psychologist etc. all require higher degrees. This has an unavoidable impact on employment league tables.

But this is only part of the story. Proving their wide range of employability skills, social science graduates work in an extremely broad range of occupations and careers, both in social science-related sectors and those which, on the face of it, would appear to have almost nothing to do with the subject disciplines.

This is particularly true for psychology graduates, many of whom find their high-level interpersonal and communication skills leading to careers in fields as diverse as banking, accountancy, career guidance and the police.

Destinations of social science graduates from 2008, six months after graduation

	Numbers graduating (survey respondents)	Entering employment	Entering further study/ training	Working and studying	Unemployed at time of survey	Other
Economics	3,480	53.1%	14.5%	12.9%	8.8%	10.7%
Geography	2,280	57.8%	19.1%	6.5%	6.4%	10.2%
Law	10,255	35.2%	40.0%	10.9%	5.5%	8.4%
Politics	3,950	54.7%	20.2%	6.7%	8.8%	9.7%
Psychology	9,635	59.0%	14.5%	10.4%	7.4%	8.8%
Sociology	4,465	62.7%	12.9%	7.0%	8.4%	9.0%
All subjects	220,065	61.4%	14.1%	8.1%	7.9%	8.5%

Source: HESA DLHE 2007/08

Task

Look at the above statistics and discuss them with your child. What do they tell you about the graduate job market? Are there any surprises – anything that might prompt you both to consider exploring other subjects? Remember that the stats quoted above relate only to very early career destinations. Within a year or two a very different picture is likely to emerge. Nevertheless, this data is useful in giving you an insight into current levels of labour market demand. What matters is how you choose to use it.

8
Why it matters where you study

There are approximately 200 higher education institutions in the UK. Of these, most are officially 'universities' – a term which for many signifies the ability to award their own designated degrees.

But don't let this fool you. Despite the common name, beneath the surface huge differences now exist between Britain's different types of university – differences in entry standards, differences in learning and teaching styles, differences in curricula, and of course, differences in employment outcomes.

G rasping each university's differences is fundamental to understanding why in today's graduate job market some graduates are automatically better placed than others, even before making it to an interview. Remember: to the uninitiated, Manchester United and Crawley Town FC are both football clubs. The well-informed, however, know the difference.

A brief note on jargon

Universities love jargon. You could say they thrive on it. To you and your child, a full-bodied encounter with university-speak can be at worst intimidating, at best, tiresome – a bit like having to learn a new computer language without a decoding key.

To help you, below is a brief summary of some of the abbreviations which still exist to fog the world of universities. You may find it useful.

1994 Group	A term used to describe research intensive universities not enrolled in the Russell Group
HESA	Higher Education Statistics Agency
HEFCE	Higher Education Funding Council for England
Post-1992 Group	A generic term used to describe institutions that became universities with the 1992 Education Act
Russell Group	The top 20 UK research-intensive universities
UCAS	University and College Admissions Service – the organisation responsible for helping students apply to university
UUK	Universities UK – the body responsible for promoting UK universities

Studying at a 'targeted' university

Despite the growth of higher education, employers still target their vacancies at a select group of universities. For some parents, this comes as a shock. Aren't all universities equal when it comes to working with employers? Don't all students have the same career chances regardless of where they study? No.

Top graduate recruiters have never been very taken by the idea that all universities are the same, or offer graduates of equal skills and intelligence. Not many would come out openly and say it – after all, why would they? But the statistics tell a different story. When it comes to the graduate job market, most of the top graduate recruiters still target a relatively small sample of universities, most of which are members of the Russell Group and 1994 Group.

This is an important point.

In 2010, the majority of the leading 100 graduate recruiters in the UK targeted their graduate job vacancies at between just 10 and 20 universities. Of these, the five most popular universities to be targeted were:

- Oxford
- Cambridge
- London (including the London School of Economics and Imperial College)
- Manchester
- Warwick.

Broadening it out further, the top 20 universities to be targeted by leading employers were as below.

Universities targeted by the largest number of top employers in 2010–11 (High Fliers)

2011	2010	University
1	4	Cambridge
2	3	Warwick
3	1	Manchester
4	2	London
5	5	Oxford
6	6	Nottingham
7	8	Bristol
8	7	Bath
9	11	Durham
10	9	Leeds
11	14	Edinburgh
12	10	Birmingham
13	13	Loughborough
14	12	Sheffield
15	15	Southampton
16	17	Cardiff
17	–	Aston
18	–	Strathclyde
19	16	Newcastle
20	–	Exeter

If your child is applying to, or studying at, a 'targeted' university (one in the above list), compared to students at non-targeted universities, they will have access to certain institutional advantages. These advantages will vary from institution to institution, but on average they will include:

- leading graduate recruiters visiting careers fairs and on-campus recruitment events

- opportunities for internships and other curriculum-related placements
- opportunities for employer sponsorship
- networking opportunities with employers who studied at the same university.

Job opportunities with larger firms generally attract higher starting salaries. This means that graduates from targeted universities can, in theory, have access to higher paid opportunities. And as more employers are now opting to recruit via placements and internships (see Part 4), students at targeted universities have other longer-term career advantages.

All this might sound fantastic. It might sound as if all your child has to do is get a place at a targeted university and, three years later, the graduate career will be in the bag. Of course, it's not quite so straightforward.

Competition remains

Just because your child is studying at a targeted university, competition for jobs will remain severe. Having employers visit your child's campus, turn up on their doorstep as it were, is a great advantage if, that is, your child is interested in the careers that they have to offer, and if they have the skills, knowledge, experience and aptitude that are being sought.

Some of the leading graduate recruiters still insist on asking for high UCAS points, which is another reason why they target certain universities – to get into these universities, you also need to have high UCAS points. In fact, to get into a top Russell Group university, it is not uncommon for students to need at least two A*s at A level.

Academically, these are actually higher grades than most professions require. It's therefore convenient for firms to target universities in which most students come ready equipped with the academic grades they demand.

The importance of geography

Besides the academic assurances employers get from targeting unis, another reason is sheer convenience. Few organisations can afford to travel up and down the UK visiting university campuses, hiring stalls at careers fairs and inputting into seminars and lectures. Post-credit crunch, a surprising number of graduate recruiters have seen their recruitment budgets slashed, meaning that less money is available for campus visits. For many universities this has been bad news, reducing the visibility of recruiters on campus.

To summarise, simply being enrolled at a targeted university isn't by itself a guarantee of a job. Your child will still need to compete amongst the best and ensure their employability is sky high (see Part 3). But it could make the career search, and procurement, a lot easier.

Studying at a 'non-targeted' university

So what happens if your child doesn't go to one of these targeted universities?

The realistic answer is they have to work harder – putting more time and effort into researching and applying to firms.

> ❝ Not going to a targeted university doesn't mean you will be unable to work for one of the leading firms; it just means that compared to students at other universities, you're going to have to make more of an effort in tracking down information, contacts and work experience opportunities. ❞

But it's also important to stress that the jobs offered by the big graduate recruiters still account for a relatively small proportion of the overall graduate job market. In fact, it's estimated that the number of vacancies offered by the top 100 graduate recruiters (firms with the largest intake of graduate jobs) accounts for fewer than 20,000 job vacancies a year – a tiny fraction of the overall graduate recruitment market.

Nevertheless, these employers exert a disproportionate influence on the job market: after all, these are the firms you'll read about in the news media; these are the firms that you'll encounter in careers fairs; these are the firms that dominate recruitment literature. The fact is they only ever account for a small slice of the overall job market.

Task

Talk to your child about the differences between targeted and non-targeted universities. Were they aware that where they study could affect how easy it is to get a job? If your child isn't studying (or going to study) at a targeted uni, ensure you have chosen a uni that takes the future of their students seriously. Find out how to do this in the next chapter.

9
How to choose a uni

Parents are incredibly important to universities, and, with rising tuition fees and growing competition, becoming more so. As such, when it comes to helping your child choose a degree course, universities are more than happy to answer your questions. The question is: when it comes to open days and other recruitment events, what questions should you ask? This section looks at the type of career-related questions you should consider asking at university open days and how, with a bit of preparation, you can dodge the spin and get down to the facts.

Of course, helping your child plan their career starts well before university enrolment. That's why university open days are so important – for you and your child.

If you're at the stage of helping your child choose a university and degree course, the university open day will be an occasion you'll be all too familiar with. During the past few years, universities have become increasingly sophisticated when it comes to hosting open days. Once, these events were a by-word for low-key informality. Aimed primarily at students, parents were rarely expected to attend. With the focus firmly on students and the student experience, the issue of employability and graduate jobs were seldom, if ever, alluded to.

Fast forward to the present day and all that has changed. Thanks to expensive marketing campaigns and high-quality PR, open days have been transformed and repackaged into glossy, choreographed, stage-managed occasions – goodbye student societies, hello Saatchi & Saatchi.

Centre-stage in these new 'happenings' are parents. Today, across the UK, parents are outnumbering students by two to one at university open days – an incredible, though not an entirely surprising turnaround bearing in mind the costs of studying for a degree. Going to university was once a decision made entirely by students. But with the onset of rising tuition fees and looming graduate debt, parents are gradually assuming a new role.

66 Suddenly, the conversations at open days are less about student night life and more about student employability. **99**

How to put universities on the spot

As we've seen, the choice of a student's degree subjects has less of a bearing on graduate jobs than most people realise. We've also seen that where you go to uni can affect your child's chances of getting a graduate job, at least with the top recruiters. But regardless of whether your child goes to a targeted or non-targeted uni, universities now have to answer questions on the employability of their graduates – and you're the people to ask them.

Aside from the glitter, the balloons, the campus tours, the New Orleans jazz bands and the armies of student helpers, university open days are just big sales events aimed at prospective customers. As soon as you see them as educational sales conventions, you get a sense of the role that you need to assume.

However, in terms of the help they provide with employability, universities couldn't be more different. Some institutions offer highly effective careers and employability services, others offer little.

Open days (and other recruitment events) are therefore an ideal opportunity for you, as a parent, to put universities on the spot.

It's like helping your child buy their first car. You research the marketplace, consult the buyers' guide, head along to one or two showrooms, talk to sales staff, perhaps even go for a test drive. But the key to making the right decision is doing your homework, reading up as much as possible on the different makes and models, checking out performances, getting a handle on prices.

A similar process applies to university open days. To make the most of these events you need to do your homework well before the day itself. Only by doing this can you make sure you know the right questions to ask. At stake is your child's career; it's simply too important to be left to chance.

This is where the analogy of buying a car begins to fall apart. When you buy a car, helping you choose are countless buyers' guides – manuals packed full of up-to-date data on prices, models, manufacturers and case histories. There's even a *Which?* guide to help you swot up on the sort of questions you should be asking car salespeople. But when you're choosing university degree courses, you're on your own.

And that's why, when it comes to employability, parents rarely put universities on the spot. They simply don't know the questions they should be asking – the big searching questions about jobs, careers and employability. The questions you and your child really need answering. For some universities this is excellent news, because these are exactly the sort of questions they don't want you to ask. It's not that they're deliberately hiding the truth, they'd just prefer it if you didn't ask difficult questions.

This has to stop. Going to university is too important, too expensive, too time-consuming and too potentially life-changing for students to continue making poor decisions based on sketchy information. It's time to take back the university open day for parents and students.

Questions you should be asking

When it comes to open days (and other university recruitment events) there are roughly four categories of questions you should be ready to ask.

1. How the university performs in job markets.

2. How the university prepares students for jobs.

3. What links are there with employers and opportunity providers.

4. What opportunities exist for work experience and other types of employability development.

To help get you started, below is a list of questions designed to help you start thinking which questions you and your child should be asking at open days. Before we get to these questions, however, some brief notes on these four categories.

How the university performs in job markets

The main way that universities are measured in terms of how their graduates perform in job markets is by league tables. These are usually published annually in leading newspapers including *The Times*, the *Guardian*, and *The Independent*.

In order to rank universities by their graduates' employability, newspapers go by data collected from an annual survey undertaken by universities, called the Destination of Leavers from Higher Education Survey – DLHE for short. DLHE records what graduates are doing six months after leaving university, how much they're earning and what level of job they're employed in – in other words, if they're in a 'graduate' or non-graduate job.

As surveys go, DLHE is robust and accurate. Newspapers use DLHE to create complicated algorithms on which they rank universities. This data can be broken down by courses and by subjects and it also allows you to compare individual universities against each other.

Asking questions about DLHE is always a good way of assessing how relevant a degree subject is to the job market. It also helps you assess how effectively an individual institution is regarded by employers. Universities that are ranked poorly by newspapers in terms of employability and graduate jobs are seldom targeted by leading recruiters. It is therefore essential to start with DLHE.

How the university prepares students for jobs

All universities will tell you that they prepare students for the job market. However, behind the bald assertion you'll find a wealth of differences.

Since 2010 all universities have employability statements published online via the Unistats website (http://unistats.direct.gov.uk/). But just because a university has a beautifully worded statement on a website doesn't mean to say that employability is a given. Your task as a parent is to ask for examples about how employability is integrated into degree courses, what it entails and whether students gain academic credit for it. A number of universities have introduced their own university employability awards or certificates. These can be very popular with employers and, as a rule, students tend to take more seriously work for which they're being assessed. As the saying goes: no marks, no motivation.

So be ready to ask questions about what happens in the university regarding employability, how seriously it's taken by different academic subjects, and whether employability is something that students have to do for themselves or whether it's timetabled in the core curriculum.

What links are there with employers and opportunity providers?

All universities will tell you they work closely with employers (after all, who wouldn't?). Employers, however, have a knack of telling a different story. Few recruiters today have the time, inclination or budget to spend the autumn term schlepping between campuses. As we saw in chapter 8, most therefore draw up a targeted list of 'chosen' institutions and focus their attention on these lucky few.

Before your child commits to a university, you need to be clear about how well that university is networked with graduate recruiters – who these firms are, what they recruit for and where they're based. Some universities have excellent links with leading national and international recruiters; others rarely, if ever, appear on their radar screens. If your child is planning to make a career with a well-known employer make sure you find out which employers attend campus recruitment events. Better still, find out how many graduates in recent years have gone on to work in big-name firms.

What opportunities exist for work experience and other types of employability development?

No question about it: when it comes to employability, there's nothing like work experience to reach the parts other interventions can't reach. In recent years, universities have realised the power of work experience both in terms of graduate employability and as an aid to recruitment.

Some degree courses have a long history of incorporated work experience; some still treat it as an exotic extra, something to be squeezed into the darkest recesses of the curriculum. Employers, of course, take a different view. No work experience, no job offer. Full stop. It's imperative, therefore, that you ask lots of questions about work experience – where and when in the curriculum it occurs, whether it's assessed or not, who organises it (in other words, are students expected to arrange it for themselves or are there placement officers in place to set it up) and is it assessed? Again, you might find universities are not forthcoming about this, so be ready with a few well-honed questions.

To help you prepare for open days, below is a selection of questions you should consider asking at the next open day you attend.

Questions parents should be ready to ask at university open days

How the university performs in job markets

- Where does your university stand in various employability league tables?
- Please could you talk me through the Destination of Leavers from Higher Education (DLHE) statistics

like for your degree courses. In particular, how many of your recent graduates were in 'graduate-level' occupations? How does this compare to your competitors?

- Which degree courses at your university have the highest and lowest employment rates?

- What sort of jobs and careers do people from different degree courses at your university go into?

- Do you carry out any longitudinal research into your graduates' career destinations? What are your graduates doing after three, five, 10 years?

- What is the average starting salary for graduates from your university? How does this compare to your competitors?

How the university prepares students for jobs

- Could you explain to me your university's Employability Statement (the one displayed on the Unistats website)?

- What is your university's position on employability? Is there a strategy or statement in place? What sort of employability entitlement could my child expect if he/she enrolled?

- Does your university operate an employability award scheme? How will the university help my child prepare for the graduate job market?

- What support structures are in place to help students with special needs develop their employability?

- What can the university do to help my child develop commercial awareness skills?
- What if my child doesn't know what career they want to do after graduation? What sort of help and advice is available? Can students access this online?
- Do your degree courses include specific employability modules?

What links are there with employers and opportunity providers?

- How well connected is the university to local and regional employers?
- Which organisations recruit most actively from your university?
- Which employers regularly visit the campus?
- What type of recruitment events does the university operate on behalf of students?
- Does the university help students find part-time jobs?

What opportunities exist for work experience and other types of employability development?

- Do your courses include work placements? If so, who organises them?

- Are there opportunities to gain academic credit for work placements?

- What opportunities are there at the university for international study or periods of international work experience?

- Are there opportunities for student volunteering? If so, who organises them and can students gain academic credit for volunteering?

- How active is the Students' Union in terms of helping my child develop extra-curricular skills?

- What services does your careers service offer? How long can graduates continue to use your careers service after graduation?

Other key things to find out before your child applies to uni

Entry standards

Universities are free to set their own entry standards and qualifications. This means that from a student's point of view, which university you go to is to some extent dependent on how many UCAS points you can offer. Not that UCAS points alone are enough to guarantee a place at your preferred university . . .

Points are not always enough

Because of the rising demand for university places, high A level scores are rarely sufficient, particularly for popular subjects. For this reason, universities hold selection interviews and other recruitment-based assessments.

Teaching or research-led?

There is a difference. Typically, Russell Group and some 1994 universities are research-intensive, meaning that if you study at these institutions you are likely to be academics whose research is recognised to be of a very high standard. If you're at a teaching-led university, on the other hand, staff may not be as research-focused, spending more time on teaching and learning. Which environment suits your child very much depends on their interests and learning style.

Location, location, location

Don't underestimate the importance of location. Where the university is based will influence the student experience. Campus-based universities can be more intimate and community-orientated. City centre universities can give students the benefit of studying in a big city environment.

Accommodation

Standards of university accommodation vary significantly across the sector. In some university halls of residence you will be amazed by just how luxurious and high-tech the rooms have become. In others, you will soon get to feel what it must have been like to have been an extra on *Prisoner Cell Block H*. Compared to previous generations, today's students are much more discerning when it comes to standards of accommodation and most expect, as a minimum, en suite bathrooms. As a result, universities are spending millions on upgrading old residences.

Learning resources

The best thing a student can do to get a head start in the job market is pass their degree. For this reason, when assessing universities, always start by exploring the learning resources – both online and 'real'. Libraries are excellent at revealing just how seriously a university takes its scholarship and research.

Task

Before attending a university open day (or similar event), take a few minutes to write down some of the key questions you would like answered. Discuss them with your child. Your joint task on the day is to obtain answers to every question on your list. If for any reason these can't be answered, ask the organisers if they can respond to you at a later date.

10

Calculating the financial benefits of your child's degree

When it comes to calculating the economic benefits of a degree, you and your child have a number of important issues to consider. But before you can make informed decisions there are several things you need to know about the link between higher education and graduate earnings. This chapter also looks at average starting salaries by subject of study, type of job and geographical location.

I f your child is considering going to university in the near future, calculating the costs will be one of your major concerns. Essentially, the costs involved with being a student break down into three categories.

1. Tuition fees (these are not paid up-front by the student but paid back after graduation over a number of years, depending on the graduate's earnings. For more information, see below).

2. Accommodation costs.

3. Living expenses.

To some extent, how much your child actually pays in these three categories will depend on which university they choose to study at. As we'll see, when it comes to tuition fees, some universities charge more than others. But it's not just the type of university that dictates costs. Where your child chooses to study also has an impact on the overall costs incurred.

To help you start to budget, the following figures will give you some idea of the costs associated with higher education. Bear in mind that these are indicative costs: the actual costs of studying at university are highly variable and change frequently depending on government legislation, cost of living and, of course, the state of the economy.

Tuition fees

In 2011 the Government proposed that all universities in England and Wales be allowed to set variable tuition fees of up to £9,000 a year.

To justify charging the maximum amount, universities need to prove that they are making concessions to students from non-traditional backgrounds (a term usually used to denote students from families with joint incomes of less than £25,000 per annum). For such students and their families, a range of bursaries will be made available which will reduce, in some cases significantly, the overall tuition fees. A National Scholarship Programme will also be available to help students from lower-income households with tuition fees and living costs.

If your child is planning to be a full-time student studying for a first degree or other higher education course, you will be able to apply for a government loan that will cover your tuition fees. And they won't have to pay this loan back until they are earning over £21,000 a year.

Accommodation

Depending on where in the country your son or daughter plans to study, costs associated with accommodation will vary, in some cases significantly. For students, London and the South-East remain considerably more expensive that northern England, Scotland and Wales.

Another factor which will impact on your child's accommodation costs is whether they decide to live in university halls. Costs for halls vary, but in the long-term, by including lighting, heating, food and other forms of support, prices can often prove very competitive.

If your son or daughter chooses to live out of halls in private accommodation, be prepared for fairly expensive deposits, and before your child signs a landlord's contract, always check the small print.

Living costs

Living costs cover things like accommodation, food and travel. These will vary depending on where your child decides to study.

If they plan to study full-time, loans, grants and scholarships are available to help with living costs. Again, how much your child receives will depend on your family's financial circumstances.

Not all costs associated with your child's degree course are related to tuition fees. Just being a student on a degree course has a cost implication. There are books to buy, field trips to go on, events to attend. Again, these costs will vary depending on which subject your child is studying.

A recent study carried out by the National Union of Students and HSBC set about compiling a league table of the most expensive degree subjects for students to study.

Top of the league table were degree courses related to mathematical sciences and computer science. Students on these courses were regularly required to find an extra £1,430 to cover the cost of books, equipment and field work.

Students taking medicine and dentistry fared slightly better. Additional costs for them were calculated at £902.16. Students on education courses, i.e. those on courses leading to teacher training, paid the lowest additional costs. These were calculated at just £432.48.

Most expensive degree courses in terms of *additional* costs (NUS / HSBC, 2009)

1.	Mathematical sciences/ computer sciences	£1,430.40
2.	Medicine and dentistry	£902.16
3.	Business and administration	£873.36
4.	Creative arts and design	£701.04
5.	Engineering	£651.60
6.	Law	£642.48
7.	Languages	£635.28
8.	History and philosophy	£558.56
9.	Social studies	£539.76
10.	Biological sciences	£539.52

Loans

Loans are available to full-time students (not those studying via distance learning) and are to help students pay for living costs (e.g. food, travel, accommodation etc.).

Students can apply for a living cost loan of up to £5,500 a year if living away from home and studying outside London. More funding is available if the student is living away from home and studying in London, and less if they live with their parents. Again, these loans do not have to be paid back until the student is earning over £21,000 a year.

And just like tuition loans, repayments will be calculated on a sliding scale and deducted automatically from wages.

Interest rates on loans

For full-time students, interest is charged at the rate of inflation (Retail Price Index or RPI) plus 3% from the date the loan is taken out to the April after your child has finished studying.

From the April after your child leaves university they will be charged:

- the rate of inflation if you earn £21,000 or less

- the rate of inflation plus up to 3% if you earn between £21,000–£41,000

- the rate of inflation plus 3% if you earn over £41,000.

Repayments will be deducted automatically each month from your child's pay packet.

The reckoning – what will it really cost?

To help you and your child prepare a budget for going to university, below is an example (and fictitious!) weekly student budget. Preparing a weekly budget is a good idea. In the first few weeks of term, universities help students think about living to a budget, but as a parent your advice and experience are invaluable.

The budget below gives you an idea of some of the costs that are likely to be associated with student living expenses.

Weekly budget

	University room in halls (shared/single)	University self-catering room	Private flat
Rent	£120–£250	£60–£125	£80
Food	£17 for lunches	£55	£45
Gas/electricity	included in rent	included in rent	£15–£18
Internet	included in rent	included in rent	£5–£10
Mobile phones	£10–£15	£10–£15	£10–£15
Laundry/toiletries	£10	£10	£10
Total per week	**£157–£282**	**£135–£205**	**£165–£178**

Source: University of Edinburgh (costs adjusted to 2011–12 prices)

Budgeting tips

To help your child stretch their budget further, the following tips are worth emphasising.

- Set yourself a weekly budget that you keep to.
- Never shop on an empty stomach.
- Buy in bulk – shop for the week, not for the day.
- At the beginning of the week, plan your meals (and stick to the plan).
- Use electricity sparingly and economically.
- Use big shops' loyalty cards.
- Make sure you shop around.
- Look out for own brand products.
- If you can help it, don't buy new. Look out for bargains.
- If you ever feel your money isn't going as far as you'd like it to, make an appointment to see your university's financial support team. At most universities, they're available throughout the week, and offer excellent (free) help and advice.

What do graduates earn?

For today's students, going to university is an investment in the future and an academic leap of faith. A lot depends on how much in the future they stand to earn. Because of this, it's essential that both they (and you) are fully up to speed with graduate earnings.

So how much do we know about graduate earnings?

The problem with salary surveys

Traditionally, much of what we know about how much graduates earn after leaving university has come from 'destination surveys'. These are large-scale research surveys carried out in the first few months after students have completed their degree courses. While data gained from such surveys is fairly robust and reliable, it has one considerable drawback: it's collected far too soon.

The very fact that these surveys take place almost immediately after graduation means that much of what we know about graduate earnings is taken from a very early snapshot in a graduate's career. Think about your first wage cheque and then compare it to your earnings after five or 10 years at work. It doesn't take long to appreciate the problem.

The good news is that despite fluctuations in the graduate job market, overall graduate starting salaries appear to have remained fairly steady.

How graduate starting salaries changed between 2003–11

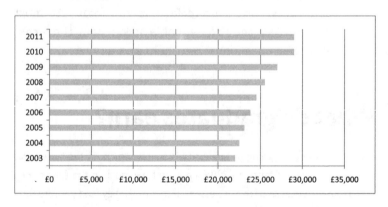

Source: High Fliers, 2011

The figure above shows average salaries quoted by employers from some of the UK's leading graduate recruiters. What this reveals is that the average starting salary for new graduates remained unchanged between 2010 and 2011.

During the recession, graduate starting salaries at the UK's top employers continued rising. In fact, median pay grew by 4.1% in 2008 and 5.9% in 2009, largely due to high inflation rates. In 2010 it looked as if the worst of the recession was over. This led to a jump in median starting salaries to £29,000.

But averages can be deceptive. Of the top 100 employers, only two were offering graduates starting salaries of £29,000 and more. Most employers started new recruits on salaries ranging between £20,000 and £30,000. Even so, these figures only reflect a small proportion of graduate starting salaries. What about those graduates who didn't find jobs with top firms?

Graduate starting salaries at leading UK firms in 2011

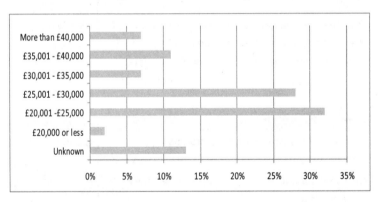

Source: High Fliers, 2011

In 2010, according to data collected by the Higher Education Statistics Agency (HESA), the organisation tasked by the government to record data on higher education, the average starting salary for new graduates was £19,677. This was 2% up on the figure recorded the previous year (£19,300).

Salaries by job sector

So how much can your son or daughter expect to earn in individual career sectors? The chart below is a summary of a comprehensive salary survey carried out recently by Graduate Prospects. This illustrates the average starting salaries for different types of graduate jobs. Given that the overall average starting salary stands at £19,677, it can be seen from the data below that the best-paid jobs are those related to health professionals – doctors, dentists and pharmacists. According to Graduate Prospects, the average starting salary for jobs in this sector is approximately £25,362.

Types of jobs	Average salary for a new graduate
Health professionals (e.g. doctors, dentists and pharmacists)	£25,362
Functional managers (e.g. financial managers, marketing and sales managers, advertising and public relations managers, personnel managers, and information and communication technology managers)	£23,976
Engineering professionals	£23,651
Business and statistical professionals (e.g. accountants, management consultants, economists)	£23,208
Information and communication technology professionals	£22,941
Architects, town planners, surveyors	£21,567
Teaching professionals (e.g. secondary and primary school teachers)	£19,989
Science professionals	£19,972
Legal professionals (e.g. solicitors and lawyers)	£19,765
Sales and related associate professionals	£19,134

Types of jobs	Average salary for a new graduate
Design associate professionals (e.g. designers, including web designers)	£17,829
Artistic and literary occupations (e.g. artists, writers, actors, musicians, producers and directors)	£17,334
Social welfare associate professionals (e.g. youth and community workers, housing officers)	£17,317
Legal associate professionals (e.g. legal executives and paralegals)	£16,931
Sports and fitness occupations	£16,443
General administrative occupations	£15,374
Customer service occupations	£14,543
All occupations	£19,677

Crucially, some sectors pay below average starting salaries. These include jobs in sports and fitness, general administrative work, and jobs related to customer services.

Postcode and earnings

How much your child earns in their career will also be influenced by where they choose to live.

As in Dick Whittington's lifetime, London remains the place to go to earn the higher salaries. Graduates working in London had a mean salary of £22,570. But interestingly, compared to every other UK region, London also generated the lowest year-on-year average salary rise. Between 2007 and 2008, graduate salaries in London grew by just 0.4%. A sign, perhaps, that London's streets are not quite paved with gold.

Scotland proved to be the best place to go for pay increases: the average salary in Scotland saw a 5.6% growth. In fact, with an average salary of £19,953, wages for new university leavers in Scotland were better than those in the south-east of England, which at the time of the survey stood at £19,561.

The chart below provides a regional breakdown of graduate salaries.

Average graduate salaries by region

Full-time, first degree 2007 graduates entering full-time employment

Region	Salary
East	£18,943
East Midlands	£17,997
London	£22,479
North East	£17,986
North West	£17,768
South East	£19,306
South West	£18,216
West Midlands	£17,970
Yorkshire and the Humber	£17,470
Scotland	£18,891
Wales	£17,655
Northern Ireland	£17,371
All UK regions	£19,300

Source: HESA Destination of Leavers from Higher Education (DLHE) 2006/07

A survey of 226 leading graduate recruiters by the Association of Graduate Recruiters (AGR) revealed how much salaries in London were pulling away from other regions. Graduates working in London for larger firms (those typically represented by AGR) were earning almost £10,000 more than those in Northern Ireland.

Salaries, however, have to be offset by other factors, such as cost of living and accommodation. Living in London is notoriously expensive and even with additional funds, graduates may find that their wages go further in other, less expensive UK regions.

Graduate starting salaries by geographical location

Location	Median starting salary (£)
London	29,000
South East	24,425
South West	23,500
The Midlands	23,140
North West	23,000
Scotland	23,000
East Anglia	23,000
Yorkshire	23,000
North East	23,000
Wales	21,000
Northern Ireland	20,166

Source: AGR Graduate Recruitment Survey 2009

The gender effect on graduate salary

Early in 2011 a report called Differences by Degree was published by two professors from Lancaster University. Working from a sample of 81,436 graduates, the professors divided graduates into five broad categories. These they termed 'STEM' (Science, Technology, Engineering and Mathematics graduates); 'LEM' (Law, Economics and Management graduates); 'OSSAH' (Other Social Sciences, Arts and Humanities graduates); 'Combined'(where more than one subject was studied); and 'A level' (non-graduates who achieved at least two A levels, but who didn't go to university). From this they went on to also examine the impact of gender and degree classification.

They showed that gender does affect graduate earnings. For example, female STEM graduates earn higher salaries than all other females aged between 21 and 30, but by the age of 40 their salaries have been passed by all female graduates except those in the A level group. Why, remains a mystery. Perhaps it reflects difficulties women in STEM careers are reputed to face when trying to combine a career and a family.

This pattern isn't replicated with women graduates from other subjects. OSSAH (Other Social Sciences, Arts and Humanities) graduates, for example, were found initially to earn less than women graduates from other subjects, but, on reaching the age of 40, overtake STEM, LEM and Combined graduates. For women, it seems that social science, arts and humanities degrees are not get-rich-quick subjects, but slow-burners.

For men, the earning profile is markedly different.

Male LEM graduates begin their careers on higher than average salaries and keep on going! In fact, the good times for this group continue rolling until the age of around 55, when their earnings finally begin to tail off. Of course, this might have little to do with reduced employability; it could be that they're starting to retire.

Male OSSAH graduates at first do better than the other three groups, but by the age of 40 have been overtaken by all male groups apart from those in the A level category. As far as men's earnings are concerned, STEM subjects don't appear to offer the same disproportionately high earnings as they do for women.

Does degree classification matter?

Again, yes. The same study found that students' degree classifications were a useful predictor of lifetime earnings. Essentially, graduates who performed better academically, once in the job market, earned higher salaries. In fact, men with low-grade social science, humanities or arts degrees actually earned less than those with A levels. This means that a man with a low-grade social science, humanities or arts degree actually earned less than someone without a degree.

Again, however, graduates from law, economics and management continued to buck the trend. Even with low-grade degrees, male LEM graduates earned above-average salaries.

Task

With your child, discuss these findings. Which category of degree subject is your child planning to study, is currently studying, or has recently graduated from? What career are they interested in pursuing? Do the findings of the study surprise you both, or is it as you expected? How important is money a consideration in your child's academic and career planning?

So will going to university pay off?

The answer is yes — but only as long as you and your child do your homework before they enrol on a degree course. As we've seen, returns on degree qualifications vary widely and are dependent on where you go to study, which degree course you opt for and where you live after graduation. Earnings are even dependent on your child's gender.

Is a degree a good career investment? Undoubtedly, yes. Our reading of the job market suggests that the world of work in the future will require more graduates – more people with high-level skills and knowledge.

But there are no guarantees. Simply having a degree doesn't automatically mean a certain level of earnings, nor does it mean access to a certain type of career. For that, your child will need to work hard, gaining not just academic qualifications but strategically important work experience. They will also need to acquire the right blend of extra-curricular achievements. And they will need to have contacts – people who can help gain them access to key networks. There's another word for this: employability.

Part 3

During university: eyes on the prize

Part 3 is all about letting you in to a secret: the secret of employability. As you read, you'll discover the skills, knowledge and experience employers will expect your child to acquire and develop while at university. In today's graduate job market this isn't optional, it's expected.

Part 3 takes you through what your child could – and should – be doing during uni to increase their employability.

11

More than a degree: the skills your child needs

There's lots that your child can do during university to boost their employability. And best of all, it won't cost anything. This section gives you an overview of what else your child should be doing while at university to enhance their CV.

In the face of record numbers of applications many recruiters are taking radical action, switching the focus away from traditional academic qualifications to broader, experienced-based selection criteria.

A new idea of 'talent'

What's becoming clear is that the days of recruiting students in the final year at university are rapidly coming to an end. As we're about to see, the search for 'talent' is forcing more recruiters than ever to switch their focus away from final-year students and to students at a much earlier stage in their tertiary education. With more students than ever graduating from university with degrees, internships and work experience are becoming the new gold standard.

By looking at employers' preoccupation with talent we can see that many of the skills and attributes recruiters use to assess it actually have very little to do with pure 'talent'. What they're really talking about are personal and cultural characteristics – qualities such as motivation, enthusiasm, commitment and confidence. They're looking first and foremost for people like them; people who fit in with their organisational values and mores, people who represent the brand, who present a positive image to external clients, people they can trust in any situation or context to always do the right thing. It's this that employers are really looking for. This is the definition of real, lasting talent.

One employer admitted as much when questioned about his bank's approach to talent management. Interestingly, as you'll see, the employer actually admits that what they're looking for isn't an expertise in banking. After all, this can be taught. What the firm is looking for, what it really values, is something far more personal, something that can't be taught, a quality or characteristic that you either have or don't have.

> ❝ Our approach is to understand the person
> profile, not the skills profile. What does this
> person need to have in their profile? We need high-
> end empathy; we need people who can actually step
> into the customers' shoes and understand what that
> feels like. We can't teach people to be more flexible, to
> be more empathetic . . . but we can teach them
> the basics of banking . . . we can teach them that
> quite easily. So we are recruiting against more of
> the behavioural stuff and teaching the skills stuff, the
> hard knowledge that you need for the role. ❞
>
> *Global HR Director, as quoted in* The global auction: The
> broken promises of education, jobs and incomes, *Brown,
> Lauder & Ashton, 2010*

Plotting the 35-hour week

Bear in mind that university students are meant to be engaged in their studies for 35 hours a week. For some students, particularly those on vocational degree programmes, 35 hours is a reasonable estimate of the amount of time spent on academic studies.

For other students, however, time spent engaging with academic subjects is far more variable. In some universities, and in some degree subjects, students might find that they have less than six or seven 'contact hours' per week ('contact hours' means the total number of hours spent in lectures and tutorials).

But this doesn't mean for the rest of the week they have nothing to do. All it means is that for the rest of the week their learning and development is in their own hands.

University isn't like school or college; students aren't timetabled for every hour of the week. They are, however, expected to engage with the wider aspects of student life. They are expected to participate in student clubs and societies, engage in volunteering and sports, join in with the wider, extra-curricular aspect of higher education. Not only do universities expect this but employers do, too.

So when discussing with your child how they spend their time at university, it's worthwhile to keep the 35-hour rule in mind. Just because a student isn't timetabled to attend lectures every day of the week certainly doesn't mean that they can relax!

Task

As a parent, you need to make sure you check with your child, on a regular basis, to what extent they are engaging with the wider, extra-curricular aspects of university life. In today's job market it's important that your child recognises that a degree isn't enough and that other skills and achievements are called for – things that can only be developed outside of the lecture theatre.

It's unlikely to make you popular – after all, few students welcome parents asking questions about how well they're utilising their time. Nevertheless, in the long term, it'll be worth it. Who knows, one day you may even be thanked!

The essential skills employers want

After several decades at the top, Sir Richard Branson remains Britain's leading business entrepreneur: a self-made billionaire whose meteoric career defies categorisation. To whom does he attribute the secret of his success? His mother and her somewhat unorthodox approach to the school run.

First, some background. Ever since they started school, Eve Branson was determined that her children would grow up independent and with the confidence to make their own decisions. This she took seriously and, as it turned out, literally.

Every afternoon, when driving four-year-old Richard home from school, while still several miles from home, Eve would stop the car and ask Richard to get out and find his own way home – unaccompanied and without a map. To add to the challenge, Eve would stop the car at different locations, thus forcing Richard to navigate a succession of different routes.

To this day, Sir Richard attributes his multi-billion pound business empire to his mother's single-minded determination to force him to think for himself – and to live with the consequences.

But don't try this at home!

Underpinning this story are two highly relevant points.

First, as a parent, you occupy a crucial role in the development of your child's work-related attitudes, skills and assumptions.

Second, to be effective, you don't have to do everything for your child; all you need to do is create the situation within which your child's learning can take place. The independence and autonomy that Richard Branson acquired, while trudging through fields and country lanes, were not passed on to him by his mother but were learnt and internalised by his own experiences. All Eve did was to stop the car and ask that he find his own way home.

As we have seen, in the 21st century the most significant challenge for graduates will be to manage their relationships with work and with learning. If they don't do it, changes in organisations mean that no-one is going to do it for them.

Skills to build

If you want to know what skills employers are looking for, you can't do better than talk to the Confederation of British Industry. The CBI know a thing or two about skills – after all, they regularly consult their members (thousands of them) to find out what skills they're recruiting for and where the gaps lie.

Essential employability skills

Recently, the CBI produced a list of what it claimed were essential employability skills. These skills, the CBI claimed, were in demand across the economy. Below is a summary of the CBI's employability skills shopping list. To what extent has your child acquired these skills and where are the gaps?

Self-management

Readiness to accept responsibility, flexibility, resilience, self-starting, appropriate assertiveness, time management, readiness to improve own performance based on feedback/reflective learning.

Team working

Respecting others, co-operating, negotiating/persuading, contributing to discussions and awareness of interdependence with others.

Business and customer awareness

Basic understanding of the key drivers for business success, including the importance of innovation and taking calculated risks, and the need to provide customer satisfaction and build customer loyalty.

Problem solving

Analysing facts and situations and applying creative thinking to develop appropriate solutions.

Communication and literacy

Application of literacy, ability to produce clear, structured written work and oral literacy, including listening and questioning.

Application of numeracy

Manipulation of numbers, general mathematical awareness and its application in practical contexts (e.g. measuring, weighing, estimating and applying formulae).

Application of information technology

Basic IT skills, including familiarity with word processing, spreadsheets, file management and use of internet search engines.

Underpinning all these attributes, the key foundation, must be a **positive attitude**: a 'can-do' approach, a readiness to take part and contribute, openness to new ideas and a drive to make these happen. Employers also value **entrepreneurial graduates** who demonstrate an innovative approach, creative thinking, offer fresh knowledge and challenge assumptions.

The importance of self-reliance

It's not surprising that self-management tops the CBI's list. Over the past few years, self-management – the ability to be able to organise your own career development – has become increasingly important. Universities are aware of this, but rarely refer to it in these terms. In higher education, we call it self-reliance.

❝❝ Self-reliance is the key to 21st century job markets. Think of it as nothing less than the secret of employability. ❞❞

Self-reliance enables students and graduates to manage their own careers, to make effective career transitions into and across the job market. Self-reliance skills help people to position themselves effectively in jobs and careers where their other skills and abilities can shine. Without the skills of self-reliance, other skills can be lost or wasted. That's why this group of skills deserves special treatment.

According to a report by the Association of Graduate Recruiters (AGR), entitled *Skills for graduates in the 21st century*, a graduate who is self-reliant should be **'aware of the changing world of work, take responsibility for their own career and personal development, and is able to manage the relationship with work and with learning throughout all stages of life'**.

So let's look in more detail at what self-reliance actually consists of. According to AGR, self-reliance consists of several sub-skills, or attitudes. These are:

Self-awareness

- Able clearly to identify their skills, values, interests and other personal attributes.
- Able to pinpoint their core strengths and 'differentiating factors'.
- Equipped with evidence of their abilities (such as a summary statement or record).
- Actively willing to seek feedback from others, and able to give constructive feedback.
- Able to identify areas for their personal, academic and professional development.

Self-promotion

- Able to define and promote their own agenda.
- Can identify 'customer needs' (be they academic, community or employer) and can promote their own strengths in a convincing way, both written and orally, selling 'benefits' to the 'customer', not simply 'features'.

Exploring and creating opportunities

- Able to identify, create, investigate and seize opportunities.
- Has the research skills required for identifying possible sources of information, help and support.

Action planning

- Able to plan a course of action which addresses: Where am I now? What do I want to be? How do I get there?
- Able to implement an action plan by organising time effectively, identifying steps needed to reach the goal and preparing contingency plans.
- Able to monitor and evaluate progress against specific objectives.

Networking

- Aware of the need to develop networks of contacts.
- Able to define, develop and maintain a support network for advice and information.
- Possess good telephone skills.

Matching and decision-making

- Understands personal priorities and constraints (internal and external). This includes the need for a sustainable balance of work and home life.
- Able to match opportunities to core skills, knowledge, values and interests.
- Able to make an informed decision based on the available opportunities.

Negotiation

- Able to negotiate the psychological contract from a position of powerlessness.
- Able to reach win/win agreements.

Political awareness

- Understands the hidden tensions and power struggles within organisations.
- Aware of the location of power and influence within organisations.

Coping with uncertainty

- Able to adapt goals in the light of changing circumstances.
- Able to take myriad tiny risks.

Development focus

- Committed to lifelong learning.

- Understands preferred method and style of learning.
- Reflects on learning from experiences, good and bad.
- Able to learn from the mistakes of others.

Transfer skills

- Able to apply skills to new contexts.

Self-confidence

- Has an underlying confidence in their abilities, based on past successes.
- Also has a personal sense of self-worth, not dependent on performance.

Task

As a parent, there's a lot you can do to help your child develop self-reliance skills without forcing them to walk long distances home from school every evening.

Look again at the above list of self-reliance skills. With your child, work through each of them, ticking those skills which you both feel your child has achieved to date. Try to put together examples of how your child might give evidence of these skills on a college or job application form.

In particular, try to focus on those skills which require further development. What's missing? How self-reliant does your child consider themselves to be? Remember: what matters isn't that your child can tick all the boxes, but that they have a plan in place for acquiring and practising as many of these self-reliance skills as possible. Try to set targets and dates by which these skills will have been obtained.

12

The employability edge – help your child stand out from the crowd

Employability isn't just about qualifications and courses. It's about being able to offer more – more skills, more experience, more commitment, more added value. This section looks in more detail at just what it is that makes employers recruit graduates: the secret ingredients that spell the difference between success and failure.

I n 2010, a major UK law firm advertised to recruit graduate trainees. The firm is one of the most prestigious in the world, with offices in all Western capitals. To apply for the job, students had to fill in the firm's eight-page application form. Of these, the first five or six pages were fairly typical, covering academic qualifications, work experience and reasons for applying to the firm.

The final section, however, under the heading 'Additional Information', gave the game away by revealing what other things employers expect when hiring today's graduates (see below).

Additional Information (law firm)

Please provide information on your contributions and achievements towards the following:

- positions of responsibility (education)
- positions of responsibility (sporting)
- academic awards
- sporting awards
- duke of Edinburgh's Award
- debating societies
- clubs and societies (formed or chair)
- young enterprise
- organisations (chaired)
- musical instruments (please indicate level of proficiency)
- languages (please specify numbers of languages spoken and levels of fluency)
- theatre performances (give examples)

- dance (include level of proficiency)
- volunteering work
- charity work
- community engagement
- travel experience (dates and locations visited)
- other . . .

It is curious to speculate on what else students might possibly be expected to add under the heading 'other' – lion taming perhaps, or winning the X-Factor? But in this, the law firm wasn't alone. Other leading graduate recruiters ask for similarly challenging lists of extra-curricular achievements.

The point is this: to land a graduate-level job, today's graduates need significantly and *substantially* more than just academic qualifications. What counts is the personal, social and cultural capital that students acquire through extra-curricular activities – things they organise and do by themselves. It's the sports played, the work experience gained during summer holidays, the clubs and societies represented, the roles and responsibilities taken on . . . it even comes down to musical instruments!

As a parent, you might find this surprising, shocking even. Recruiters however, are unapologetic. The sheer imbalance between the supply of graduates and the demand of employers means that every year the bar is raised. Last year's exceptional becomes this year's average.

> **“** We recruit up to 1,500 graduates on to one of our 70 graduate programmes around the world. For those jobs, globally, we receive around 100,000 applications. As 90% have a 2.2 or a 2.1 and will therefore meet our criteria, it takes something extra to stand out. Recent recruits include a graduate who taught English and Spanish in Guatemala; one who ran a restaurant; another who worked in the

Beijing Paralympics; a Punjabi singer who's been on TV. Another graduate from Cameroon had published a book and set up a small business selling second-hand clothes from New York to Africa, before joining HSBC. **"**

Stephen Green, former Group Executive Chairman of HSBC, speaking in 2009

Read this extract again, carefully. You've just overheard one of the world's leading CEOs disclosing what it takes to get a place on his company's graduate recruitment scheme. From this admission, the following points are worth briefly dwelling on.

- HSBC's 1,500 job vacancies are advertised not just in Britain but around the world.

- The company runs 70 graduate training programmes every year, across the globe.

- For these 1,500 vacancies, the firm expects to receive around 100,000 applications (that's 66 graduates competing for every job).

- Of these 100,000 applicants, some 90% will be offering exactly the same academic qualifications. In other words, for the majority of graduates, having a good degree is no longer a differentiator, but a given. A degree will no longer guarantee you a job but it will give you a chance to compete.

- To be successful, graduates need to have obtained *extraordinary experiences* and *stand-out skills*, nearly all of which they will have organised outside of university.

Not all experience counts!

As you'll note from Stephen Green's words and the law firm's 'Additional Information' questions, when it comes to assessing which type of extra-curricular activities or achievements count, employers, like everyone, can't avoid making *assumptions*. The reason for this is straightforward. Nothing we do exists in a historical or social vacuum. Everything we do has a history, and attached to that history are various cultural indicators. These indicators reveal certain things about us – about where we're from, about our family background, about what sort of expectations we have for ourselves and our children.

That's why you'll find that when it comes to graduate recruitment, when listed on a CV, some sporting achievements are more effective than others. As one employer has said:

> ❝ Tennis and rowing exhibit energy and contribution, playing snooker does not. ❞

Another employer, a recruitment manager from a large professional services firm, when asked to give an example of the sort of experience that would go down well with her firm, offered the following example:

> ❝ I've met graduate interviewees who have done some wonderful things, like going on jungle treks in their gap year! ❞

Of course, not all students and their families can afford a jungle trek in their gap year (not all can afford a gap year). Such examples show, however, that cultural achievements count and that when it comes to assessing students' extra-curricular achievements, some are definitely more highly regarded than others.

Why employers insist on extra-curricular achievements

As already noted, extra-curricular achievements are important to employers because they offer a useful and efficient way of separating out applications. Employers also stress that recruiting students who have gone the extra mile, organised their own placements, stood for positions of responsibility, and made every effort to develop additional skills, is simply good for business. People who stand out in university generally stand out in the workplace. As one recruiter said:

> You can spot people who've been active in sports clubs or have taken part in lots of union-linked activities where they've been treasurer or secretaries and where they've had to get on with everybody, organise things, produce books to account for their funding. When you meet people like that they have this little bit extra.

For you and your child, it's essential that you spend time thinking about the extra-curricular achievements that your child will be able to offer employers. Once, graduate employability was dependent on 'hard currencies' such as qualifications and work experience. Today, while such things still count, 'soft currencies' such as interpersonal skills, appearance, dress style and even accents, are increasingly coming to the fore. As one study on the new realities of the graduate job market has argued:

> Dress, deportment, speech, skiing holidays, hobbies and interests are all incorporated in the creation of a personality package which must be sold in the job market.

Task 1

Working with your child, see how many of questions in the law firm's 'Additional Information' section you both could complete. Remember: it's a tall order, and few graduates can provide evidence against all questions. But what does your child's extra-curricular profile look like – and how might they gain additional experience?

Task 2

Ask your child to look at the following list. Working together, how often do you both carry out the following activities? (Score: 1 = Never; 2 = Hardly ever; 3 = Sometimes; 4 = Often)

- Watching TV current affairs programmes
- Reading books unrelated to educational studies
- Going to art galleries or museums
- Going to the theatre
- Attending classical concerts
- Keeping up to date with current affairs
- Playing an instrument
- Playing a sport
- Reading a quality newspaper
- Attending a debating club or society
- Attending a public library
- Volunteering in the community
- Attending evening classes
- Working in a part-time job
- Going to new places, meeting new people

Look at your scores and discuss them with each other. If the maximum score possible is 60, how did you score?

Gap years: making them work

Gap years are popular with students for a number of reasons. Not only do they offer a period of respite between A levels (or the equivalent pre-university qualifications) and higher education, they have also tended to be popular with university lecturers. Young people entering university with more life experience under their belts are often found to make better, more committed students.

Even employers have tended to look favourably on the gap year, seeing it as a year's worth of valuable work experience and skill development.

But all this was *before* the credit crunch.

Since the downturn, the value of gap years has come under increased scrutiny. As we've seen, employers are becoming increasingly choosy about what type of work experience they're looking for. In a crunched job market, experience of any type of work is less marketable than *strategically relevant* work experience – that is, experience gained with relevant organisations, key competitors, even within the organisation itself. This is the experience that really counts. Everything else is second best.

Even the value of travel isn't what it once was. In the 1990s, travelling the world was sufficiently rare to make it a key selling point to put on a CV. Today, that's no longer the case. Blame it on cheap air tickets and economic globalisation, but travelling isn't necessarily the guaranteed career boost that it once was.

So is it the end for the gap year?

Not necessarily. Gap years can still be effective – both in terms of helping young people mature and develop, and in enhancing their long-term employability – but only if care is taken to ensure that the year is spent developing the employability skills discussed at the start of this section.

Task 3

If you want to assess how marketable your son or daughter's proposed gap year might be, try considering the following points.

Gap year guide

- Has the gap year been carefully planned – with clear aims and objectives?
- Has the gap year been planned around pre-identified times and dates?
- Does your child know exactly what they will be doing directly after the gap year?
- Has the gap year been discussed with your child's tutors and careers advisers?
- Will the gap year lead to the development of key employability skills (if so, which)?
- As it progresses, will there be a chance for your child to review the gap year?
- If travel is involved, are you both clear how this experience will enhance your child's employability?
- Will the gap year enhance your child's commercial awareness? If so, how?
- Will the gap year make your child a better university student? If so, how?
- Is the gap year likely to lead to additional skills, experience or insights?

13
Work experience

The issue of work experience is rarely out of the news. Like crude oil, the economic downturn has sent its value spiralling. Once, work experience was viewed as an optional extra, something that came second to a student's academic qualifications. Now it enjoys equal billing, as important on a CV as any degree or diploma.

This chapter takes a closer look at work experience – how it works, why it's so important and the practical steps that you as a parent can take to boost your child's career options.

On the face of it, there's nothing *all that* mysterious about work experience – people have been engaging in it for centuries. How else could skills and knowledge be passed from one generation to another? In education, however, work experience can often mean something more specific.

One of the best definitions of work experience has been put forward by the Quality Assurance Agency – the organisation whose task it is to ensure that schools and colleges do what they say they're going to do. Work experience in a QAA context, means:

> ❝ ... a planned period of learning, normally outside the institution at which the student is enrolled, where the learning outcomes are an intended part of a programme of study. It includes those circumstances where students have arranged their own learning opportunity with a placement provider, with the approval of the institution. ❞

The key word here is *planning*. Nothing differentiates good and bad periods of work experience nearly as much as planning. It's also the easiest thing to get wrong.

Depending on what stage in the educational process your child is at, you'll have a range of different work experience options and opportunities available. The key point is that you don't have to assume that the only work experience available to your child is the work experience organised by their school or college. Many parents assume this to be the case, so it's worth saying again: when it comes to organising your child's work experience, you don't simply have to rely on your child's teachers.

To a large extent, when it comes to organising and administering work experience and in terms of helping your child learn from the experience, no one is ever quite as effective as *you, the parent*.

The DIY work experience

So how do you do it? How do you build a work experience programme for your own child, and without resorting to schools and teachers?

The first thing to do is relax. Contrary to what you might have read in the press, in order to give your child a head start in the job market you don't need to have Richard Branson on speed-dial. Such stellar contacts can help, but for most families success starts closer to home.

In fact, it starts *at home*. The best people to help you organise your child's work experience are people around you: family, friends, colleagues, neighbours, relatives (distant and near), even semi-acquaintances. Once, you might have thought of them as a friend, a relative or a work colleague. Not any longer. From now on, they're potential leads.

Next, make a list. With your child, write down the names, job titles and employers of as many people you know and who you can comfortably approach for a favour. You're looking to identify as many people as possible who, through their jobs, careers, networks and contacts, can provide your child with a brief period of work experience. This doesn't need to be hands-on work experience, it could be work shadowing (i.e. observing other people in the workplace), it could even be work sampling (trying out small aspects of a particular job). Whatever the type of experience, what counts is that your child gets a direct insight into a particular aspect of the world of work, which helps them when making career decisions and can be used on application forms and CVs as evidence of commitment and motivation.

Who do you start with? Easy – people with whom you're most familiar. Family, friends, social contacts, perhaps even people who you know through work. Keep in mind you're looking not for world famous chief executives or cabinet ministers, you're looking to identify people who, through their skills, contacts, networks and jobs can offer your child an opportunity to gain a period of work experience.

Don't even worry if your contacts don't work in jobs or sectors in which your child is interested. At this stage, your priority isn't to get your child a job, it's simply to give them experience of the workplace – a chance to gain valuable skills and insights.

Take time drawing up your network. Chances are, you'll be surprised at how many people, together, you both know.

Next, it's time to prioritise. Draw up your top three to five potential opportunity providers. These should be people you know and who offer the capacity for providing useful work experience. They should also be people who you can speak to without jeopardising friendships, relationships or careers. Not that what you're about to do is in any way illegal, but it's always good to make sure that you've got all the bases covered.

To help you prioritise, ask yourself the following questions.

- **Is the person you are considering in a position to offer useful work experience?**
- **Would this experience offer the chance to gain a practical insight into an important aspect of working life?**
- **Would this experience come with the chance to gain employability skills, e.g. self-reliance skills, communication skills, team-working and commercial awareness?**
- **Does the person work in a job or organisation that is relevant to your child's future career goal?**
- **If it were possible, would the work experience be accessible and convenient?**
- **Would you, as a parent, be able to return the favour (e.g. might you be able to offer work experience to the contact's children?)**

This last question is worth pausing on. Being able to offer reciprocal work experience for someone else's child in your own job or organisation is one of the best ways of securing work experience for your child. Call it 'intern trading' or simply Normal Human Behaviour – it's one of the most powerful ways that parents can help boost their children's work experience.

> If you've never considered this, now's the time. Because it's happening all around you: parents have been trading internships and work experience opportunities between themselves for years.

Making contact

Once your top choices are in place, the next step is to make contact. There are essentially two ways of going about approaching people for work experience opportunities. The first is undoubtedly the easiest. You do it yourself: you phone, write, email, visit or doorstep a contact to ask if it might be possible for them to let your child spend some time with them gaining work experience.

Option two: your child makes the first contact – again, via letter, telephone call, visit or email. This is harder because few young people have the confidence to do this on their own. But flip this on its head, and that means if your child does make the first contact, they will immediately stand out from the crowd. Already, they will be practising the very skills you want them to acquire and develop.

> Remember, not all work environments are suitable for young people, and you may need to take professional advice about insurance and liability cover.

Introducing the foreign land of 'work'

Work experience has two big advantages. First, as we'll see in the next section, being able to evidence periods of work experience on a CV or application form is always highly effective. In fact, once a prospective employer has checked out your child's academic qualifications, the section on the CV headed 'Work Experience' will probably be the next thing they turn to. Indeed, so important has experience become, that some recruiters *begin* with work experience then move on to educational qualifications.

But looking good on paper is only one of the advantages to be accrued through work experience. If properly organised, it's the best way to give young people a direct insight into the ever-changing world of work.

This second point is easy to overlook, particularly if for the past two or three decades you've been submerged in working life. Just because *you* know what it's like to work in an office or factory or design shop, it's easy to think that your son or daughter must somehow have acquired a similar insight into working life.

In fact, for many young people the world of work has become an increasingly strange and unfamiliar foreign land complete with its own language, culture, conventions and terminology. For outsiders, trying to decipher this world gets harder every year.

Scan through a job vacancy website and try to put yourself in your child's position. How many job titles would they recognise or aspire to? Welcome to one of the biggest problems with today's world of work. The gap between young people's career aspirations and the actual jobs on offer in the job market has never been wider. Making things even more difficult is the new crop of titles which employers use to describe jobs. How many young people, for example, aspire to be systems analysts? How many human resource consultants? *C++ programmer,* anyone?

But it's not only job titles that are alienating young people from the world of work. Work itself is vanishing out of sight. Many jobs today either take place behind glass windows or are carried out in cyberspace, where they are invisible to all but a select few. Mobile technology and the internet are recreating work into something which requires only limited physical interaction with fellow human beings.

For young people this presents a problem. If you're unable to watch people as they go about their daily work, how are you supposed to find what it's like to do different types of jobs? If you've no idea what a 'professional services consultant' does (they're an accountant), or a 'financial services adviser' (banker), or wrongly conclude that a 'mission control analyst' must do something involving NASA (they don't; they too work in a bank) how can you possibly begin to make your own career decisions?

The answer is work experience, the ultimate passport to the new world of work.

The weird world of job titles

Ever heard of the following jobs? All job titles are genuine.

- Generic DIP practitioner
- Waste management disposal technician
- Head of inspiration
- Direct debit administrator
- Collections and recovery adviser
- Surround mastering engineer
- Local land gazetteer custodian
- Street naming and numbering officer
- Field force agent
- Surveyorship enumerator
- Family protection consultant
- Coordinator of interpretive teaching
- Mission control analyst
- Process operative
- Vertical engineer
- Welcoming agent (otherwise known as a receptionist)
- Wet leisure assistant

Source: BBC

No experience, no job

In addition to demonstrating motivation and commitment, work experience has other benefits. For some professions, such as law and accountancy, relevant and recent work experience isn't an option, it's essential. One recent survey found that over 50% of all new graduate jobs were reserved exclusively for those who had had work experience placements with law firms. There are signs that other professional sectors are not far behind. In instances such as these, work experience isn't just a vehicle for gaining an insight into a particular career, or a useful thing to put on one's CV; firms use it as a way to weed out so called 'weaker' applicants.

---

10 benefits of work experience

1. Improved confidence and maturity
2. Better understanding of the workplace and what it takes to succeed
3. More information on which to build career decisions
4. Contacts and access to social networks
5. Enhanced self-awareness – better understanding of personal likes and dislikes
6. Improved academic results – students with work experience often prove to be better (and more committed) learners
7. Opportunities for part-time jobs
8. Chance to develop employability skills, such as problem-solving, team working, and communication skills
9. Insight into what employers really look for when recruiting
10. 'Heads up' on future opportunities.

Types of work experience to look out for

It's taken a while, but education has finally woken up to the benefits of work experience. From schools to university, work experience is a common feature in most curricula. That's not to say, however, that the spectre of useless work experience has been banished entirely from academia. It hasn't. Unfortunately, far too many examples of poor quality work experience placements are still dotted around the sector, wasting everyone's time and generally giving the initiative a bad name.

So, briefly, what makes good work experience?

In the diagram below is a checklist of what makes good work experience. Of course, it's not exhaustive, but it will give you an idea of what work experience should include.

Remember, work experience isn't just something that's arranged as part of a course. Some of the best work experience is organised and administered by students and parents working either in partnership with a school, college or university, or by themselves.

Educational stage	Work experience examples	Who's the organiser?	What's the payoff?
High School (Years 10+)	Part-time job	Pupil or Parent	Valuable experience combined with financial gain
High School (Year 10–11)	Formal work experience placement	School and Parents	Valuable experience, integrated into curriculum
High School (Years 10–12)	Duke of Edinburgh's	School and Parents	Valuable experience; counts towards DoE award
Sixth-form / Further Education college	Formal work experience as part of course	Tutors – usually by relying on links with industry	Valuable experience and might contribute towards final award
University	Student volunteering	University careers service or student	Experience in some cases may count towards degree
University	Student placement	University careers service, academic department or student	Placements are usually accredited, therefore count towards degree
University	Placement year	Either University department or student	Placement years count towards final degree qualification
University	Part-time jobs	University careers service, students' union, or students	Rarely accredited, but provide financial remuneration and the chance to develop employability skills
University	Internships	Usually advertised by careers service but increasingly 'traded' between parents, students and employers	Work experience often paid at reasonable rates; chance to develop specific skills and experience

Work experience checklist

- The work experience project or placement is well organised, with clear, up-front objectives.

- Overseen by a named person, who has experience in administering work experience projects.

- Complies with all relevant Health & Safety legislation.

- Resonates at some level with the student's career aspirations or ambitions.

- Fits in or is relevant to the student's curriculum or subject of study.

- Arranged at a convenient time for both the student and provider.

- Counts towards an academic grade.

- Involves undertaking a project or study.

- Students can undertake them in partnership with other students.

- For the duration of the placement or experience, the employer will nominate a named member of staff who is both experienced in administering work experience placements and is conversant with Health & Safety legislation. This person should also understand the aims and objectives of the placement.

- During the placement or experience, the young person should be visited at least once by a member of school or college staff. Not only is this a good way to review progress but it can also help deal with any problems or emerging issues. If a visit isn't possible, a telephone call should take place.

- Upon completion of the placement or experience, a debriefing exercise is essential. This should take place as soon as possible and should follow a structured format. Participating in this debriefing exercise should be the young person, the employer (or their representative) and a member of staff.

14

Internships

Since the economic downturn, a new type of work experience has come to prominence: internships. But what constitutes an internship – how do they work, and while on one, should your child expect to get paid?

Faced with a shrinking job market and rising graduate applications, it didn't take long for government ministers and UK universities to realise that a new approach to graduate recruitment was urgently called for – an approach that would give large numbers of students direct contact with the job market even if it was only for a short period of time. Hence the new popularity of internships.

What is an internship?

An internship is essentially a period of work experience arranged for a graduate or university student. Internships can last for flexible periods of time – some last for up to a year, others for just a month or two. The idea of an internship is that it's like a job but designed for someone with limited (or no) experience. Think of it as an insight into a specific career or occupation, a way of gaining practical, hands-on skills and knowledge without actually committing to, or being hired for, a full-time job.

For students and graduates, the benefits of internships are legion. Not only do they gain valuable experience and skills but good internships can lead to the forging of numerous contacts which can in turn be used to gain access to new job opportunities. For employers, the benefits are more business-like. Internships are an ideal way of recruiting top graduate talent while keeping the permanent headcount low. In times of economic uncertainty, bosses like to keep the labour force flexible, and no job is as flexible as an internship.

So far, so good – until, that is, the subject of money crops up.

The issue of whether or not internships should be paid, is one of the most controversial and contentious questions in today's graduate job market. On both sides, feelings run high. Some people think that internships – as periods of work experience – should never attract a salary. Others argue that because they're aimed at graduates and entail actual (not made up) work, it's only fair that they should attract a wage. In some highly competitive industries such as the media, a long history exists of not paying interns regardless of how many hours they work or what tasks they're required to undertake. Because employers know that demand for media internships will always be high, with or without pay, few are prepared to start paying interns.

Should your child take on an unpaid internship?

Before your child starts exploring internships you need to have a careful conversation about whether or not they will accept unpaid opportunities. In recent years, the number of unpaid internships available to graduates has dramatically increased. This poses lots of problems.

> ❝ Unpaid internships 'cost' those who do them real hard cash – both in terms of actual expenditure and in potential earnings. ❞

Unpaid internships can be incredibly difficult to sustain. After all, it's estimated that simply going to and from the workplace every day costs most people at least £10. On top of this are lunches and appropriate business dress – all of which have to be paid for. Unpaid internships, no matter how you look at them, cost money, only this time it's not the employer who's paying but the employee.

On the other hand, supporters of unpaid internships maintain that these can be effective if the experience being gained is utterly vital to a future career choice. In such cases, they argue, internships should be looked upon not as a cost but as an investment – one that in future years will yield handsome returns. Either way, it's essential that your child is clear about the pros and cons of internships and can pay the price.

The following guidelines might help you and your child come to a decision.

- **Hours of work**. An unpaid intern should have no formal set hours of work (e.g. 9am–5pm). If they do, it's a job and therefore ought to be paid at an appropriate rate.

- **Management structure**. Unpaid interns are, effectively, volunteers. Therefore they should have no formal management accountability. Nor is the intern under any obligation to stay with an organisation for any set period of time.

- **What's the deal?** If an internship starts as unpaid, both parties ('employer' and intern) should be clear about how long the internship will last and what, on both sides, is the 'deal'. In other words, the 'employer' needs to know what they can expect from the intern, while the intern should be clear about what level of skills or training they will receive in return.

- **Brief encounter.** Internships shouldn't really last for more than a year. If they do, they're in danger of straying into full-time job territory. At the same time, internships that last for less than a month or two can often be too short to benefit either side. Again, being clear at the outset what each party expects to gain from the internship can pay dividends at a later date.

How to arrange an internship

Since the economic downturn, universities across the UK have become deeply involved in organising and administering internships. Many of these are advertised on university websites and are available for students on graduation. There are also various national and regional websites on which internships are advertised. For more details, see www.prospects.ac.uk.

But these are the minority. The majority of internships are never advertised on websites or displayed in careers services. They're filled without most graduates ever finding out about them. How they work and how they're distributed is increasingly dependent on the use of networks and contacts.

Organising an internship is remarkably similar to the steps taken when organising work experience placements (see Chapter 13, Work experience), and once again is all about using your existing contacts. The difference between these is the issue of pay, and you may find it hard to broach the subject of whether your child could enter into a paid internship. However, it never hurts to ask, or to suggest even, and it's vital to establish whether it will be a paid internship at the start, if your child will only consider a paid position.

Part-time jobs at uni

Internships aren't the only way to get work experience while at university. For many students, experience of work and the chance to develop employability skills comes from part-time jobs.

Part-time jobs are incredibly popular with students, mostly because of the additional income they provide. For their part, most universities are happy for students to work during their studies (in fact, there's even some evidence to suggest that students who work on a limited basis during their studies often go on to receive better grades). But even amongst the most tolerant institutions there are limits to how many hours students are advised to work. Generally, the advice is that during term-time, students on full-time degree courses should work for no more than 15 hours a week. During holidays and vacations, these hours can be relaxed. During term-time, however, it's essential that students' part-time jobs don't distract them from their academic studies.

This might sound like an obvious point to make, but it's worth stressing how important it is that students don't lose sight of the need to make sure that part-time jobs remain just that — part-time. As pressure on finances becomes ever more acute, increasing numbers of students are now spending longer hours in the workplace. Many will tell you they have no choice. Nevertheless, establishing a balance between part-time jobs and academic studies is essential.

One way to do this is to recommend that during term-time your child spends no more than 15 hours a week working in a part-time job. The rest of their timetable should be spent on academic study. And remember: a student might not be timetabled to spend all their 35 hours a week in lectures, but this doesn't mean that they're not expected to be working towards their degree.

Students' part-time jobs come in many forms, ranging from the traditional student jobs in pubs, restaurants and hotels, to the less common jobs in offices and businesses.

❝❝ **Employability-wise, those part-time jobs from which students can gain commercial awareness skills are generally highly valued by graduate recruiters, as are those from which students can accrue problem-solving and other business-related skills, such as time-management and communicating with customers. ❞❞**

Jobs in which commercial awareness can be developed tend to be those in which employees manage budgets, generate income or maximise sales revenues. I recently met a student who worked part-time in a local petrol station. In the height of winter, he noticed that sales of anti-freeze were lower than expected. He therefore took a decision to stack cans of anti-freeze prominently in the garage forecourt. As a result, sales rocketed — resulting in an unexpected bonus and, for his CV, a fantastic real-life example of commercial awareness.

To help students arrange part-time jobs, most universities now run some type of student job shop either on campus or via the university website. These are highly popular and, depending on the time of year, usually stock lots of part-time job opportunities.

And remember, part-time jobs have another long-term advantage. Not only do they help students gain extra cash, they also help them accrue employability and direct experience of the workplace – two essential commodities in the competition for graduate jobs.

Task

Discuss with your child the issue of internships. Depending on their career plans, how important or useful might an internship be? What sort of internship might be considered? How would your child go about organising it?

Part 4

Getting that job

So far, we've looked at the forces that are reshaping the graduate job market and the skills, knowledge and aptitude that successful applicants are expected to display. Now for the final section – the part when we look at the tactics and strategies your child will need if they are to get a job. This part looks closely at what it actually takes to help your child get a graduate job: applications (CVs and application forms); networking; information interviewing; the importance of business cards; and how you as a parent can help your child succeed at assessment centres.

15
Finding jobs to apply for

We've covered what your child will need to increase their employability levels, but how do they go about finding jobs to apply for? Where are the best jobs advertised, and how does your child ensure they are the first to know about them?

Before we look at the tactics you'll need to acquire to help your child succeed in the job market, let's consider talent.

The talent wars

Talk to any graduate recruiter and it won't be long before they mention the 'T' word. Since the late 1990s, talent has been a major obsession in the HR community. Talent management, talent retention, talent fast-tracking, talent spotting . . . never have so many resources been harnessed to such an elusive and subjective concept.

It all started with a report written in the early 1990s by the management consultancy McKinsey. Entitled 'The War for Talent' the McKinsey authors described 'talent' as the grit in the oyster of any successful organisation, the one factor that could differentiate a firm from its competitors:

> " In the boardroom bunkers and in the cubicle-filled trenches, the early skirmishes of the next war are being fought. For the moment, most of the action is guerrilla warfare – brief raids in which the companies under attack are often unaware that they've been hit. Ultimately, though, the war will be global, and for businesses, the stakes will be success and perhaps even survival. "

For HR managers, this was incendiary stuff. Within months, leading graduate recruiters around the world were reviewing (or writing) their own 'talent strategies'. Foremost in their minds was the idea that despite the massive increase in the numbers of graduates pouring into the job market year after year, actual 'talent' was finite – a limited commodity, a flawless diamond in a world of paste and cheap reproductions.

Spotting who was officially 'talent' and who wasn't became a global preoccupation among leading employers. As a result, it wasn't long before a sort of 'talent apartheid' arose between the two groups – those with 'talent' and those without. Employers themselves recognised that defining both groups could be a difficult, even unpleasant, process. As one HR manager told researchers for a study undertaken in 2010 for Praxis:

> ❝ We have segmented our employees brutally just in terms of talent. They've gone through quite a tough assessment process . . . We have this group who are recognised as 'talent' and this group who are recognised as 'not talent'. And that group that are talented, we actively manage in terms of how long they have been in their current role, what's their next role? They get moved around the world quite a bit. They get stretched and put 'out there'. ❞

As far as graduate recruiters were concerned, *more* graduates meant *less* real talent out there on the market. Their task, therefore, was to fight to win the best talent; to compete with other graduate recruiters to make their own recruitment schemes as attractive as possible to genuine 'talent', while at the same time devising ways to reduce the amount of time spent reading and sifting through 'non-talent' applications. Graduate recruiters were at war – a War for Talent.

Finding those graduate jobs

Like other types of jobs, graduate jobs are increasingly to be found advertised on the internet. But don't let this fool you. Despite the use of modern technology, when it comes to timetabling and planning, some things never change. During the 1970s and 1980s, in graduate job terms, the 'milk round' referred to a series of visits made by graduate recruiters each year to leading universities. These employers would travel to campuses early in the morning (hence the name) to carry out a series of job interviews and assessments. If they were successful, students could be offered jobs on the spot.

Today, the traditional milk round no longer exists. Increasing use of the internet has made it possible for employers to advertise and recruit without leaving their premises. But old habits die hard. Take, for example, employers' closing dates.

One of the most important points that careers advisers have to get across to final-year students every year is how early employers' closing dates are. How early? Well, let's assume that a student returns from summer vacation in September. Almost immediately, graduate job vacancies will start to be advertised by employers, specifically targeting final-year students. In most cases, these employers will be recruiting a year in advance; they won't actually be expecting the final-year student to start work with them until the summer of the following year.

Despite that, most of these job vacancies will have closing dates well before the Christmas vacation, meaning that final-year students have just two or three months to research, prepare, write and submit graduate job applications. After Christmas, most vacancies with leading recruiters will have expired. Even though they will have six or even seven months to go in university, for many graduate job-hunters it will already be too late.

Employers claim that early closing dates are needed simply in order to process the many thousands of applications they tend to receive. The longer job vacancies remain open, the more applications they will attract.

But in practice, there's another reason. Research shows that the best applications usually arrive early in the recruiting process, with the poorer quality ones arriving later. Employers know this, which is why they set early closing dates. That's why it's essential that you make sure your child always applies for jobs well in advance of closing dates.

Where are graduate jobs advertised?

Job vacancies for graduates can be found in a range of locations. The first place to start searching is via the university's careers service website. Usually, your child will find here a range of vacancies and opportunities, many targeted at their own degree subject.

Following this, there are the national job sites. In recent years, organisations like Graduate Prospects (www.prospects.ac.uk) have developed extensive UK-wide vacancy sites, holding job vacancies from a broad spectrum of industries and sectors. Access to the Graduate Prospects website is free although students have to register online to use it.

Not all graduate job vacancies are online, however. Unique to higher education, a number of publishers each year send job directories to university careers services, which students can pick up for free. These directories are packed full of thousands of job vacancies and lots of useful information on the graduate job market and leading recruiters. Your child's careers service will be best placed to advise them about the best directories and brochures to collect.

Examples of these publications include: *The Times 100 Employers* (High Fliers Research); *The GTI Target Jobs Guide; Real World*; and *Prospects Directory*. Be aware that individual universities may not stock all these publications.

Another source of graduate job vacancies is university careers fairs and other such recruitment events. It's worth emphasising that these can be very effective for giving students direct access to graduate recruiters, while also providing a direct opportunity to gather application forms, recruitment brochures and other useful information on graduate job opportunities.

While these events are targeted predominantly at final-year students, students from other years often find them very useful in obtaining an early insight into the recruitment market. It is never too early to start the research.

Recruitment and selection

Once students have obtained graduate job vacancies, the next stage is to go about applying. And as they do so, without them knowing, they enter the world of graduate recruitment and selection – a world full of complexity and tradition.

It's at this stage that the graduate job market takes a swift detour from other job markets. For in order to be offered a graduate job, particularly one with a leading organisation, applicants must go through a series of assessments, tests, interviews, assessment centres and group exercises. There's an expression for these tests and assessments which neatly sums up what they aim to achieve: 'weapons of mass rejection'.

These recruitment exercises have been designed to reduce the pool of applicants until only those who meet the recruiter's aims and objectives are left.

The table below shows the most popular selection exercises currently used by employers when recruiting graduates. You'll see how, over the course of a decade, the use of different types of exercises has changed. Some, like the use of different types of tests, have proliferated, while others, for example, the use of paper application forms, have diminished. What you'll see, however, is just how complicated and potentially difficult it now is to get a graduate job.

Percentage of employers using various selection techniques when selecting graduates

	1999	2009
Only accept online apps	2%	76%
Only accept paper apps	98%	2%
Telephone screening	10%	40%
Online exercises	2%	36%
Personality tests	35%	64%
Numeracy tests	25%	80%
Verbal reasoning	23%	71%
Assessment centres	21%	79%

As a parent, your task is to help your child prepare for and succeed in the recruitment exercises. To help you, several points are worth making.

- Online applications are rapidly becoming the most common form of application method, with paper-based applications (and letters) becoming a thing of the past. Online applications present their own unique challenges, as any parent who has been frustrated by the use of 'text-speak' will testify.

- Telephone interviews are becoming increasingly popular for several reasons. Tele-interviews are cheap and efficient and they can also be outsourced to call centres and other mass-volume operations.

- Tests take many forms, but suffice to say that 50% of all UK degree holders fail psychometric tests (tests designed to be taken online or via paper-based assessments). The term 'psychometric tests' actually covers a wide range of tests; some are based on assessing personality, others on typical IQ tests (numeracy, literacy, verbal reasoning, etc.) Again, just being in possession of a university degree is no guarantee (or indicator) of success, which is something that graduates often find hard to accept.

• Assessment centres are often used at the final stage in the recruitment and selection process. Sessions can last for between half a day and two full days. Usually comprising formal tests, group exercises, presentations, team challenges and formal interviews, the assessment centre is the nearest thing your child will come to finding themselves on the TV programme *The Apprentice*.

The next few chapters show you how you can help your child through each of these recruitment exercises and prove to a graduate recruiter that they possess not just the academic skills and abilities to fit into their organisation but also come equipped with the interpersonal skills and attributes which ultimately separate success from failure.

16

Applications, CVs and covering letters

No matter how good your child's academic performance is, success or failure in the job market is dependent on the ability to write effective job applications. And with employers spending less than two minutes on each application, there's no room for mistakes. This chapter tells you all you need to know to help your child write winning applications.

W hen it comes to writing CVs and job applications, in the words of Alexander Pope, a little knowledge can be a dangerous thing. As a parent, you're no doubt used to making applications and writing a CV. After all, it's how you probably got your job. But a word of caution: when it comes to graduate CVs and applications, things have changed. Once, applications could afford to be relatively generic; today, they need to be forensically tailored to every single opportunity.

> " Before the crunch, job applications were like cricket bats – you used the same one no matter who you were playing. Today, think of them as golf clubs. To get through a round, you need to master a bag full of different clubs, each with its own unique role and function. "

This section looks briefly at all you need to know about the art of writing graduate applications so that you might use this knowledge to help your child. Who knows, it might even help you the next time you come to apply for a job!

CV: RIP?

If it were an animal, the humble curriculum vitae would by now be on the endangered species list. In recent years, changes in its natural habitat – i.e. the graduate job market – have seen its numbers falling dramatically. Once, CVs were almost the only way that students could apply for graduate jobs. Now, thanks to the internet, the CV's old hunting grounds are being rapidly colonised by the more aggressive, quicker breeding online application form.

But while CVs are no longer in demand by the same number of employers as they once were, knowing how to write a CV, just in case it's needed, is an essential career management skill and in itself a useful exercise. After all, what other experience forces you to condense your skills, qualities, work experience and academic achievements into two sides of A4?

How to write a CV

The first thing you need to be very clear about, when it comes to helping your child with their CV, is that a CV isn't really a document of one's life (despite the Latin insistence to the contrary) but a hard-nosed sales document. A CV is to a job-seeker what a car brochure is to a car showroom. Because most people forget this simple fact, employers complain that the average CV is about as interesting as reading a telephone directory.

Finding a USP

The idea of the USP is taken from the advertising and marketing sector where it's often used when trying to position a new product in a crowded market. A good USP makes a product (or, in this case, job-seeker) distinctive, unique and relevant. It also makes the reader want to find out more.

A CV with no USP is destined for an early encounter with the office shredder. After all, unless an employer is able to ascertain quickly and easily what the applicant's unique selling point is, it's unlikely they will take the time to work it out for themselves. There just isn't the time available.

What comprises a unique selling point depends on what type of job or employer the CV is being addressed to. To resonate and be effective, a USP has to relate to the priorities and objectives of the reader's organisation. So to help your child work out what their USP is, spend a few minutes thinking carefully about what the target organisation's business needs are, the issues they're currently facing and what priorities they discuss in their application brochure and recruitment website. Your child's USP should aim to address some of these priorities.

The USP could be therefore a particular skill your child has acquired (such as experience of team work, being a proven problem solver, being proficient in a foreign language), an experience (perhaps an internship or work experience placement in a particularly relevant industry or sector) or an achievement which marks them out as special. For most young people, their greatest achievement to date is related to education – qualifications, prizes and school or college-based experiences. Used sparingly, these can be effective in contributing towards a USP. Remember, however, in today's crunched job market, qualifications alone are unlikely to constitute a USP.

Don't worry if it takes some time for you and your child to identify a USP – at first, few students and graduates find the concept easy. But it is definitely worth persevering.

Putting the CV together

Traditional CVs were pretty directionless compilations of facts, dates and addresses. But in today's job market, when few CVs receive more than two minutes' worth of scrutiny, CVs have to be concise and to the point. Anything longer than two sides of paper is the CV equivalent of *War and Peace*.

Remember, CVs are now sales documents, designed to promote and market the writer's unique selling point. Their goal is to win a place at a job interview.

How CVs should look is, to a large extent, in the hands of the writer. There's no blueprint for the perfect CV. This is an important point, particularly if you haven't found yourself applying for jobs lately. You'll be surprised at how much CVs have changed in recent years, largely as a result of the influence of advertising and marketing.

The following information provides an overview of some of the key points related to CV-writing.

Format

Two sides of A4 paper are generally regarded as the maximum length for most graduate CVs. Anything longer than two sides of paper is a dangerous gamble and unlikely to go down well with time-pressed recruiters.

Paper quality is important (i.e. avoid cheap photocopy paper) but not so important that you should only use expensive parchment paper. The aim of the CV is to make it look and feel professional.

Font

Too much ink has already been spilt on speculating about which fonts work best when writing job applications. While it's never a good idea to get obsessive about a choice of font, from a simple design perspective time spent thinking about which font works best for your son or daughter's application is rarely wasted. Fonts, in case you hadn't realised, have their own personalities: Times New Roman – safe, traditional, little bit dull. Arial – businesslike, modern, easily accessible. Always resist the urge to use comic fonts. There's nothing remotely funny about them.

Layout

When thinking about layout, remember to make sure that your child appreciates that the top third of the first page is, from a reader's point of view, the most valuable part of the CV. It is to here that the reader's attention will naturally gravitate and where their attention will be at its peak. From then on, even the most attentive reader's attention will start to wane. To make a lasting impact it's essential that the information presented in this part of the CV is the most marketable part of the document: the USP.

To do this, think of a headline – a powerful, leading story. For many people, this means a short, introductory 'Career Aims' paragraph, in which key achievements and attention-grabbing announcements are made. For others, it's an academic qualification or period of work experience. Whatever it is, a powerful CV needs an effective headline.

Also remember that as far as CVs are concerned, the amount of space allocated to an event or achievement indicates its overall level of importance. More space: more importance. And vice versa. Encourage your child to think carefully about how much space is allocated to different sections.

Tone and structure

It might sound strange, but from a reader's point of view every CV has its own 'tone of voice'. Getting the tone just right can be harder than it might seem. Many CVs suffer from 'sounding' too formal and official; others can easily come across as too casual and relaxed. So it's important to work with your child in establishing the right tone of CV voice. Rather than casual or over-officious, you want to aim for businesslike and professional.

How the CV will be structured is also worth spending time thinking about. Unlike application forms, there is no blueprint for a CV – as long as the key points are covered, they can follow any design template.

Below is a list of key points to consider when writing CVs.

What's the lead story?

If your child's CV is to grab and keep the reader's attention, it needs a lead story – a key point around which the rest of the information flows. In most cases, the lead story will be your son or daughter's USP.

Relevance counts!

If they're going to avoid the shredder, CVs should be relevant to the employer and the job vacancy in question. It's therefore always a good idea to try wherever possible to reflect the target organisation's priorities and goals. For exactly the same reason, this is what makes speculative CVs so ineffective – they're just too general to be convincing.

Establish the right tone of voice

Talk to your child about the CV's 'tone of voice' – does it sound too meek and apologetic, or too egotistical? It's essential that your child feels comfortable with the look and feel of the CV; after all, they'll be the one facing the interview panel. My advice is to avoid superlatives and hyperbole, no matter how tempting. A bit of modesty always goes a long way, even if it's false.

Personal information

CVs are personal advertisements, not exhaustive lists. For that reason, it's up to the writer to decide how much personal information to include. Some personal information such as name, address, email and telephone number(s) is non-negotiable. Other information, however, depends on the writer. Once, CVs regularly featured gender, date of birth, even marital status. Today, few CVs go into such detail.

Third person wins

There's a chapter in *Ulysses* when, to encourage his readers to think about Homer's Cyclops episode, James Joyce uses the first-person 'I' as frequently as possible (Cyclops, you'll recall, only had one 'eye'). The result is a chapter peppered with 'Is'. CVs which rely heavily on the first-person singular eventually end up reading like bad James Joyce: 'I worked', 'I studied', 'I travelled' and so on. To avoid this, try using the third-person 'it', as in 'It was a three-month internship'. It's more businesslike, it's more readable and it makes the CV read more smoothly.

Career synopsis paragraph

To help increase the impact of CVs, more students and graduates are now using a 'career aims' paragraph. Often included at the top of the document, just below the personal information section, a career aims paragraph can be an effective way of introducing the CV's Unique Selling Point both quickly and efficiently to the reader. Think of it as an executive summary, providing the reader with a useful and concise synopsis of the applicant's skills, experience and ambitions.

Reverse chronology

Instead of presenting information chronologically, encourage your child to approach the CV in reverse chronology – i.e. listing the most recent (and relevant) events and achievements first. This makes the CV look immediately more relevant and up to date.

Curricular, co-curricular and extra-curricular

Remember that employers want to hire people who are rounded and effective in a range of contexts. For that reason, your son or daughter's CV needs to include achievements and successes gained not just as part of a course of academic study but also as part of their wider co-curricular and extra-curricular activities. It's here that extra-curricular achievements work well – Duke of Edinburgh's awards, playing for sports teams, representing college and university, leading clubs and societies.

Credential challenge

If your child is in university, chances are they will have a long list of qualifications. If this is the case, a dilemma inevitably arises over which qualifications to put in and which to leave out. GCSEs can cause a particular dilemma. Perhaps the best way to approach this is to encourage your child to put themselves in an employer's position. Most recruiters want to read about degree subjects at the expense of GCSE subjects. So it's worth allocating more space to higher qualifications, and less to those from school. My advice would be to summarise GCSE qualifications thus:

10 GCSE (grades A-C) including English, mathematics and science

Grades

No rules exist to dictate whether A level (or other) grades should be included on CVs, but of course, leaving grades off might lead to further questions. If your child's grades are less than sparkling, think about using the following wording: 'A level passes in French, sociology and art'.

Proofreading

This is where you as a parent can really make a difference to a CV's success or failure. Spelling mistakes on CVs are unforgiveable and totally avoidable. Before your son or daughter sends out any applications, make sure you proofread them carefully.

> **❝❝** Remember, gone are the days when people needed one CV to last them throughout their career. Today, CVs should be targeted at individual job vacancies. Think of them as being like golf clubs. A different one is needed for different shots. **❞❞**

For more advice on writing a CV, take a look at *You're Hired: How to write a brilliant CV* (Trotman, 2009).

Task

Together, why not help your child produce a draft version of their CV? The sooner you do this, the better as you'll be surprised how long it takes to develop an effective CV. Once a working draft exists, ask people to comment on it. Offer £5 to anyone who can spot a spelling mistake. If they do, it'll be money well spent.

Covering letters

When helping your child apply for jobs, it's also important that they understand how to write effective covering letters. In today's world of work, the term 'covering letter' also covers any email that accompanies a CV or application on its journey to a recruiter. Many young people treat covering letters or accompanying emails too casually, spending all their time working on the CV or application and treating the text which accompanies it as an afterthought.

It gets worse. With the introduction of text messaging, when applying for jobs growing numbers of young people are now using text-speak or text-spelling, signing off emails with 'C U soon' or even, in one case, a smiley face symbol.

Of course, as far as employers are concerned, such innovations rarely result in a happy ending. Bad covering letters and poorly written emails rarely make it past the shredder. Even more are deleted without ever making it on to paper. Who's 'LOL' now?

So make sure your child isn't fooled into thinking that a covering letter or accompanying email needn't be treated with anything less than total concentration. It might sound like a relic from the Victorian age, but anything you send to a potential recruiter has to be of the very best quality.

The following points should help you cover all bases.

First things first

The aim of a covering letter is to tell the reader exactly why, in as brief a format as possible, the applicant thinks they are the right person for the job; nothing more, nothing less. Think of it as a trailer to a Hollywood film: it makes you want more, but if it leaves you wanting to switch off, it's failed in its mission.

Length

Covering letters need to be brief and to the point. One side of writing paper is the maximum length – anything longer risks fatiguing the reader even before they've got to the CV (surely a classic job-seeking own goal if ever there was one). If it's an email, three or four paragraphs at the most. Remember that emails need to be even more concise, particularly given that people generally find it harder to read a long email when it arrives on screen.

Write to a named person

Unless your son or daughter is applying via an anonymous application process, where, in the interest of equal opportunities, names are omitted, aim to always get a name. This is particularly the case when writing covering letters. Begin with a person's name, while always trying to avoid using 'Dear Sir or Madam'. Tip: to find out who is the best person to write to, in my experience, company receptionists are a fantastic mine of information.

Format

Remember, the aim of a covering letter is to introduce the CV and set the scene for what's to come. It therefore needs to be concise and to the point, offering a brief summary or overview of your child's main achievements and skills. For this reason, it's often a good idea to use bullet points to summarise key ideas.

Grab attention

Covering letters, like any marketing documents, need to catch the reader's attention. There are a number of ways of doing this, e.g. highlighting periods of work experience or relevant academic studies. Again, this is a perfect opportunity for emphasising the USP.

Who makes the next move?

Finally, make sure the covering letter ends with a statement of intent. In other words, the letter should make clear what the job applicant expects to happen next. If the expectation is that the employer will make the next contact, make sure the letter says this. Leave nothing to chance: the prize at stake is too important!

Application forms

Despite all the talk surrounding CVs, most graduate recruiters now require job-seekers to complete some kind of online application form. The bad news is that few of these are as straightforward as they appear. In fact, students often complain that they're harder and take longer to complete than academic assignments. This section looks at graduate application forms and how you as a parent can help your child compete better on paper.

In the graduate job market, application forms are rapidly overtaking CVs as the main vehicle for job applications. Each year, graduate recruiters spend large amounts of money on improving and finessing their application forms. Nevertheless, the typical application contains several reasonably predictable sections.

- Personal information section with name, address, email contacts, telephone number etc).

- Academic achievements – GCSE, A level, AS level, other qualifications.

- University education: title and duration of degree; expected or final degree classification; name of university; dates of attendance.

- Personal achievements; positions of responsibility; membership of clubs and societies; travel; volunteering.

- Work experience: job title; employer; dates and duration; skills gained.

- Personal competencies. Usually a list of essential competencies is listed, such as team-working, communication, problem-solving, commercial awareness. Alongside each, applicants are required to give examples of when they have demonstrated these competencies.

- Extra-curricular activities: membership of clubs and societies.

- Additional information.

Remember, the application is only the first stage of the application process.

A timely warning

One leading graduate recruiter warns applicants:

'First of all, you'll complete an online application form. You'll need to register for the specific area you're interested in. There are also a few competency-based questions which should take about an hour.

'Secondly, we'll set you a numerical/verbal test [. . .] You'll need to set aside around 20 minutes for each test.

'After this, we'll hold an interview over the phone which should last around an hour. Again, it's competency-based, so make sure you have solid examples to substantiate all you've said on your application form.'

This highlights an important point, and one which many students overlook. The application form isn't just a one-off — something that gets you to an interview. It's the basis on which many interviews are held. Think of it as an examination script which you write yourself.

Raising the bar: blame it on search engines

The plain fact is the internet has made it no longer possible for job-seekers to plead lack of information on application forms. Thanks to the digital revolution, no matter which organisation your son or daughter might be preparing to apply to, you can guarantee that the internet will have pages and pages all about the firm's management structure, its attitude to corporate social responsibility, its shareholders – even the lifestyle and salary structure of its CEO.

This means that when reading application forms, recruiters expect to encounter well-constructed, brilliantly informed, completely up-to-date synopses of their organisation. Anything less won't be tolerated. In fact, it'll be deleted.

And when it comes to today's graduate job market, the vast majority of application forms *are* deleted, often within hours of arriving in an employer's inbox. To understand why, try putting yourself in a recruiter's shoes. In May 2011, I met with a recruitment manager for one of the UK's oldest and most prestigious retail organisations. That year, the firm recruited 16 graduate trainees. In total, by the time the closing date arrived, 2,500 applications had been received. In other words, 156 graduate application forms for every job vacancy. In her words:

> ❝ As the closing date loomed, we were receiving 50 to 60 application forms a day – all from graduates. And there were just two of us in the office! Just to keep up with them we had to carry round piles of applications, reading them wherever we went. Whenever someone called by the office we'd ask them to help do some selecting. We got through them all, but eventually you do find you develop a sixth sense. You very quickly get to work out which applications

are good, and deserve an interview, and which you can reject. Many of those we rejected just hadn't done their homework – it stands out a mile. **"**

Recruitment manager at a leading UK retail organisation

Doing your homework is the key to graduate application forms. To the expert recruiter, applicants who haven't carried out enough research into the job and organisation are easy to spot and reject. Perversely, in a market in which the supply of graduates far exceeds the number of jobs on offer, submitting a poor quality application form could actually be doing a hard-pressed recruiter a favour!

So how can you make sure your child's job application forms are as strong as possible?

Below is a checklist for writing winning applications.

- Make sure they read everything they can get hold of about the job, the firm/employer, the industry, profession or sector they're applying to. If your son or daughter is a graduate, they will be expected to be fully conversant with current affairs and any news items related to the prospective employer. Make sure they read a quality newspaper.

- Applications should always be written with one eye on the employer's website and recruitment literature. Highlight the key skills, qualities, attitudes and experiences that the organisation is in the market to hire, and make sure your child's application fits the bill.

- For added impact, try to ensure the application reflects aspects of the recruiter's business terminology, jargon and vocabulary.

- Make sure dates and factual information are precise and accurate.

- Simple, factual, straight-to-the-point writing always beats flowery, long-winded prose. Write in proper sentences. Avoid clichés like the plague.

- At key points in the application, make sure the organisation's name is mentioned (but within reason). If done sparingly, such strategic name-checking can be a highly effective way of demonstrating to a reader that an application is worth reading.

- Every word in a job application form should count. Any padding or needless prose needs to be ruthlessly edited. Every answer, every statement, has to reflect the employer's competencies and recruitment needs.

- Observe the rules: keep to word counts, heed instructions.

- Get them to apply early: research suggests that even though employers set closing dates, applications which arrive early have a better chance of resulting in an interview than those which arrive late. Sometimes, so overwhelmed are employers with applications that they close their recruitment rounds well before the official closing date.

Task

One of the most important tasks you as a parent can do to help your child's career is to proofread their applications. They might be a PhD in English, but spelling mistakes, dodgy grammar and poorly constructed sentences will torpedo any application. You won't be thanked for it, but buy yourself a big red pen and get correcting. LoL? Don't think so.

17

'Lord Sugar will see you now': preparing for interviews

Although much has changed in the world of graduate recruitment, for many young people the job interview remains the ultimate challenge, the final stage in the journey to the job market. This section explores the graduate job interview and provides you with a first-hand insight into what it's like to be interviewed by a leading graduate recruiter.

T alk to any group of students and they'll tell you what they fear most about job-hunting is the prospect of being interviewed. In this, they're not alone. For most career novices, interviews remain a thoroughly unnerving prospect.

As a parent, there is lots you can do to help your child prepare for job interviews. For a start, you can convince them that, with preparation and focus, there's really nothing to fear. As with CVs and application forms, once you know what employers are looking for, interviews are fairly straightforward and even predictable.

This chapter gives you a brief overview of how you can help your child prepare for job interviews.

The 30-second rule

The first point you need to know about interviews is perhaps the most important and least appreciated:

> ❝ Regardless of the length of an interview, most recruitment decisions take place within 30 to 60 seconds. ❞

Some people find this assertion controversial; after all, shouldn't employers use the full length of time allocated to an interview in which to decide whether or not to hire?

In some cases they do. But this only usually happens when an employer is close to hiring a candidate but, in the back of their mind, has some reservations. Perhaps they have another candidate in mind and they're trying to think through a tie-break.

For most interviews the decision to hire is far more clear-cut. Within a few seconds of the opening question, it seems that the majority of recruiters have decided on whether or not they'll be offering the candidate the job. Once they've made up their mind, the rest of the interview is used for assembling reasons to justify the initial decision.

We make these decisions all the time – at work and in social situations. And what's interesting is that in many cases, these initial hunches turn out to be highly accurate. Not only are we psychologically disposed to trust our intuition, but in the vast majority of cases it doesn't let us down.

As normal human beings, employers and graduate recruiters are no different from anyone else. They too can't help making rapid unconscious decisions about those they interview. The only difference is that when they do make these decisions, it's someone's career that's at stake.

The question is: how can you, as a parent, make sure that your child is the one who gets selected?

Preparation essentials

As soon as your child receives the invitation for an interview, the preparation begins. Success at interviews is 80% preparation and 20% presentation. To help you help your child prepare for an interview, work through the following checklist.

- Is it clear to you what skills, qualities and experience the employer is looking for? If not, re-read everything you can get your hands on about the job, the organisation and its strategic goals. Is it apparent what sort of person the organisation is looking for? How does your child fit the bill?

- Is your child clear about their USP? Do they have a list of their top skills to hand?

- How long is the interview scheduled for? You can tell a great deal about the format of the selection process by checking how long your child has been invited to attend. If they are required for more than a couple of hours you should warn them to expect either several interviews or short selection tests. A full day makes it almost certain that the format will include interview(s), tests and assessments. If the recruiter hasn't specified what's planned, ask!

- Who's leading the interviewing? Depending on their role and responsibilities, different people give different styles of interviews. HR managers tend to focus more on general information: academic achievements, knowledge of the organisation; previous work experience, etc. Section heads and departmental managers tend to ask questions more attuned to their specific job roles.

- Who's doing the assessing? Remind your child that they are likely, on the day, to be assessed by a range of people and not just those sitting across the interview table. In many firms, each person that a candidate encounters during the interview day has an input in the final selection decision. Being offhand to receptionists and clerical staff can have literally life-changing consequences (and is rude as well).

- What's the format? Few interviews today follow the same pattern. Some interviews are conducted by two or three staff; others consist of panels of up to eight people. Your child needs to be ready for any format that might arise.

Striking the right tone

Several studies have been published recently which prove just how much, at job interviews, recruiters are influenced by their own subconscious minds.

One study found that regardless of academic qualifications and work experience, candidates who seemed to have pleasant or winning personalities were almost always at an advantage over those who seemed less friendly. This might seem obvious, but to the recruitment industry it's a revelation.

For years, graduate recruiters have been searching for the secret of objectivity – the ability to recruit applicants without admitting the influence of personal bias. Research, however, suggests that for as long as human beings are in charge of making the hiring decisions, scientific objectivity is going to remain as elusive as ever.

There are several ways that you and your child can use this information to your advantage. First, you can learn from the best. Successful candidates, researchers have found, don't just possess the right skills, experience and knowledge; they make sure that by looking enthusiastic and motivated they create a psychological bond with the interviewer.

Likeability goes a long way in interviews. In fact, according to one psychologist, likeability is more important than academic achievements and work experience. Your son or daughter can have superb qualifications and work experience but if the person interviewing doesn't feel they are someone with whom they would want to spend time working, they're unlikely to get the job.

In that case, how does anyone facing an interview become likeable?

According to psychologist Professor Richard Wiseman, there are several ways that candidates can boost their likeability during interviews.

- Find something you genuinely like about the organisation and share your opinion on it with the recruiter.
- Smile and tell the interviewer how pleased you are to be offered an interview with that organisation.
- Be prepared to give the interviewer a genuine compliment.
- If appropriate, be prepared to chat about a topic unrelated to the job that you and the interviewer find interesting.
- Make sure that you show you are interested in the interviewer and the organisation. For example, ask about the type of person they are looking for and how the job fits into the overall organisational structure.
- Be ready to show your enthusiasm about the job and the organisation.
- Maintain eye contact with the interviewer. Give a good, positive handshake.

You'll notice from Wiseman's tips that some of these aren't things that can actually be put into words. That's because true likeability isn't conveyed verbally but through body language.

Body language

Seventy per cent of the information we take in about each other is non-verbal. It's all to do with body language – the silent language of communication. During an interview, for both interviewer and candidate, body language assumes a whole new level of importance. Interviewers, determined to recruit the right person, focus intently on not only what the candidate says but how they say it. In fact, if you talk to an interviewer directly after an interview and ask them to recall their impressions of the candidate, invariably they'll talk about how the person came across, whether they seemed confident or not, the level of enthusiasm and commitment displayed, and how this person made them feel. All of these are essentially impressions, gained through a (conscious or unconscious) reading of non-verbal signals.

This is because when it comes to interviews, it's not what you say that counts, but how you say it.

Top 10 tips

Here's how your child can project positive body language.

1. **Smile!** Smiling is the best way to convey confidence and a positive attitude.
2. **Hands.** The hands are a super-highway for conveying feelings and emotions. Using your hands to emphasise a point is a powerful way of communicating. However, be aware that hand gestures can also emphasise other less welcome emotions, like nerves and anxiety. If you're not doing anything with your hands, a good idea is to keep them loosely crossed on your lap. This also prevents the interviewer from noticing if they're shaking or not.
3. **Use open gestures.** Crossing the arms is a classic defence signal and is often interpreted as a sign of being tense, uncomfortable or withdrawn.
4. **Keep eye contact.** Nothing worries interviewers more than a candidate who refuses to establish eye contact. What are they hiding? Why do they seem so shifty?
5. **Don't overdo eye contact!** And nothing unnerves quite as much as the candidate with unbroken eye contact!
6. **Refrain from touching the face.** Touching the nose or face while answering a question is a classic signal that the speaker is about to be economical with the truth.
7. **Relax.** Encourage your child to relax their shoulders and to get comfortable. Not only will it make them feel better but it will make them look more confident.

8. **But don't over-relax!** Remember, this is an interview; candidates need to look at all times alert, interested and involved. For that reason, it's a good idea to lean forward slightly. Not only is this a good way to emphasise a point, but leaning slightly forward can be an effective way of registering interest and commitment.
9. **Have a firm handshake.** A firm and positive handshake is essential. Make sure you practise handshaking with your child so that they are confident when shaking hands.
10. **Nerves.** For most people, nerves are an integral part of job interviews. Emphasise to your child that feeling nervous is perfectly normal and something that most employers will take into account. If your child is worried about being nervous, encourage them to practise mock interviews either with their careers adviser or with friends. For many people, the more they get to practise interviews the more they learn to manage their nerves.

Preparing to answer interview questions

Once your child has prepared for the interview, the next thing you should do is get them to practise answering mock interview questions. Fortunately, when it comes to asking interview questions, employers are remarkably predictable. One estimate claims that around 80% of questions asked at interviews are standard (and therefore predictable) questions. This means interview questions needn't be as threatening or daunting as they might seem.

It also means that time spent with your child practising interview questions can generate impressive results.

When helping prepare students to answer questions at interviews, careers advisers often use the STAR model.

STAR stands for:

S: situation: describe the situation

T: task or problem: what dilemma or problem did you face?

A: action: what action did you take?

R: result: what was the result of your action?

As mnemonics go, STAR is a very useful method for helping students plan how to go about answering questions. For example, if an interviewer asks a candidate to describe a situation when they had to overcome a problem, a useful way of answering might be to begin by describing the situation, setting the scene, before moving on to discuss the problem or task itself.

The next step might be to give a brief overview of the action taken – what the candidate did in response to the task or problem.

Finally, and most crucial of all, the candidate has to finish by explaining what the outcomes were of their actions and what the result was. This stage is often the part that candidates forget to add – an omission which can easily reduce the impact of even the best answers.

Once your son or daughter has grasped the STAR approach, it can be a useful way of structuring answers, particularly those which call for a more in-depth, considered approach.

Question time

Sample questions to practise

For the past few years, I have been collecting interview questions (some people collect stamps . . .). Fortunately, this isn't as eccentric as it might seem. Gradually, I have been able to put together a list of the most predictable questions asked at graduate job interviews. This list is particularly valuable when helping students prepare and practise for interviews.

No interview, in my experience, has ever asked all the questions at once – it would take hours! But many, regardless of the job sector or industry involved, include at least one or two of these questions. This makes them fairly robust and dependable.

I would recommend to you that before your son or daughter has an interview, you both spend some time reading through these lists and trying out some questions and answers. It doesn't have to be very formal; after all, few have any particular right or wrong answers.

But having your child practise answering some of these questions is a great way of stilling pre-interview nerves. It's also a brilliant opportunity to try out different ways of constructing answers.

One way of approaching this could be to work through each section, choosing one or two questions from each block. When finished, take a few minutes to reflect on the experience: which questions did you both feel were the toughest to answer? Which went particularly well?

Some of these questions your child might find reasonably straightforward. Others, however, are notoriously challenging. A few old chestnuts you might even recognise from your own experiences of being interviewed.

Remember to stress to your child that interview answers should never be memorised (no one wants to recruit a robot), nor should they be batted away nonchalantly. Employers want candidates to think carefully about the questions and to reflect on their answers. Never bluff or exaggerate; if the answer is 'I'm sorry, but I don't know', so be it.

Finally, please also stress to your child that, in my experience, I have never encountered an employer who asks trick questions. That's another urban myth. Employers want students to do well at interview. They really are on the candidate's side.

And if at the end of the interview your child isn't offered the job, tell them not to worry. As we've seen in this book, the competition for graduate jobs is so intense that all students, at some stage, will fail to get through interviews. What matters isn't that they were unsuccessful, but how they pick themselves up and get on with the task of applying for the next job.

Failure at interview stage, if learnt from, is never wasted experience.

Warm-up questions

- Tell me about yourself.
- Tell me about your life.
- What should I/we know about you?
- What are your main achievements to date?
- What is in the headlines this morning?
- Where do you want to start?
- Why am I talking to you?
- Why us?
- Why do you want to work for this firm/organisation?
- Why do you want this job?
- Why should we take you on?
- What can you do for us?
- What do you know about this industry?
- What can you contribute to this industry?
- What is your impression of this firm/industry?
- What are the major issues facing us at present?
- Who are our major competitors?
- In your view, where do you think we stand in our industry?

- How could we improve our present standing?
- What is our chairman's/Chief Executive Officer's name?
- What is our share price this morning?
- What is it (what projects are we involved in) that appeals to you?
- Who else have you applied to?
- How did you hear about us?

Questions relating to academic courses and qualifications

- Why did you choose to study those courses?
- Why did you choose to study at that institution?
- Was your college your first choice?
- What relevance has your degree/your qualifications to the real world?
- What extra-curricular activities did you become involved in while at college?
- What have you gained from your qualifications?
- Do you think students should be expected to pay for their education?
- What employment-related skills did you pick up while studying?
- What relevance has your degree/your qualifications to our firm/this job?
- What has your degree/qualifications really taught you?
- How has your vacation work contributed to your career aspirations?

Questions specifically about the candidate

- What are you looking for in your first/next job?
- How do you see your career developing over the next five years?
- Why do you think you will be a success in the position you are applying for?
- Which newspapers do you read?
- What time management strategies do you use? Do they always work? How do you prioritise?
- What things annoy or upset you? What makes you lose your temper?
- How do you deal with problems? Give examples.
- How would your best friend (or worst enemy) describe you?
- What is the most difficult thing you have ever had to deal with?
- Which historical figure(s) do you most identify with? Why?
- When have you had to introduce change in your work/life/course? Tell me about it.

Criteria-based questions

- Give an example of when you have contributed to the workings of a team. What is your preferred role in a team?
- When have you had to provide a solution to a complex problem? What did you do and were you successful?

- Give an example of when you influenced the work of others. What did you do? How did you achieve it? What were the outcomes?

- When have you been responsible for the actions of others? Give examples. What was your role? How did you overcome any difficulties?

Direct challenges

- What are your weaknesses?

- What are the situations that you find hardest to handle? Give examples.

- How can you account for your low A level grades/ GCSEs/degree/HND?

- Why did you leave your last job?

- How would you feel working for someone older/ younger than yourself?

- What skills and qualities do you need to improve and how do you intend to achieve this?

- How geographically mobile are you?

- How much do you expect to be paid?

- If you were me/us, what would you look for in a candidate for this post?

- How soon could you start?

- To make sure we get a good picture of you, what else should we know about you?

- What is your criterion for measuring success?

- If you were the CEO of this organisation, what would you do first?

- Give an example of when you had to deal with
  difficult people. How did you handle the situation
  and what strategies did you employ?

Scenario questions

As questions go, scenario questions call for a slightly different approach, one involving clear thinking and a certain amount of imagination. In general terms, scenario questions ask you to put yourself in a certain situation – a situation manufactured by the interviewer (one that usually involves a problem or challenge) and then to describe the actions you'd take to solve it. Often, with scenario questions, no right or wrong answers exist. What the interviewer is really looking for is how the interviewee goes about tackling the problem and the stages that they go through to reach the solution.

Below are some standard scenario questions that graduates in recent years have found themselves encountering.

- You are the manager of a large supermarket. It is
  5pm on Christmas Eve. The store is full to capacity
  with shoppers. Suddenly there is a power cut and
  the store is plunged into darkness. What do you do?
- You are the brand manager for a well-known
  confectionery firm. One day you are sent a note
  telling you that some of your brands have been
  intentionally contaminated with a lethal substance
  before leaving the warehouse and being dispatched
  to the retail outlets. What do you do?
- You have been put in charge of introducing car
  parking charges for staff working in the organisation.
  How would you set about tackling the situation?

Questions for the recruiter

Good interviewers allow a space for candidates to ask the interviewer or the interviewing panel some questions. Candidates shouldn't feel under pressure to ask questions; if all the questions have been answered during the selection procedure, they should say so. However, to show enthusiasm and additional research, it's often a good idea to have one or two questions prepared. Questions about further training or career development usually go down well, but questions about holidays, car parking arrangements and company disciplinary procedures are usually best avoided!

Remember to stress to your child that interviews are an excellent opportunity for obtaining clarification on certain points, such as career advancement, training and future responsibilities, and they can be a useful vehicle for making a positive impression with senior management.

The following may give you an idea of the sorts of questions your child could ask at an interview.

- Where could I be in five years' time within the firm?
- What have previous graduates gone on to achieve within the organisation?
- What are the company's plans for the future?
- What further training can you offer me?
- What are the conditions of service? (If not already specified)
- Is there a staff appraisal system in place? How does it operate?
- How frequently would I meet with my line manager to review my progress?
- What sort of induction programme have you planned for the new post?

- Who would I report to on a daily basis? What is that person's key function?
- When can I expect to hear from you? How will you contact me?

For more advice on interviews, take a look at *You're Hired: Interview* (Trotman, 2009) and *You're Hired: Interview Answers* (Trotman, 2009).

Final word: competency or strengths-based interviews?

Over the past decades, graduate job interviews have undergone a fundamental rethink. From the mid-1990s onwards, competency-based interviews have been in vogue. These are interviews in which the focus was on trying to assess as far as possible the extent to which a candidate's skills and competencies match those of the job vacancy.

Competency-based interviews were meant to be the final word in job interviewing. By focusing on *objective* competencies rather than *subjective* personal characteristics, they were supposed to be the fairest, most scientific method of interviewing.

So a typical question in a competency-based interview, might be, 'Give me an example when you displayed team-work skills'. Such predictability made them comparatively easy for students to plan and prepare for. Questions and answers were exchanged with neither enthusiasm nor spark. Overnight, recruitment interviews became a two-way recitation of pre-prepared scripts.

Unfortunately, for all concerned, competency-based interviews could also be deadly dull — the recruitment equivalent of speaking to an automated answer machine. By limiting themselves to pre-set lists of competency-based questions, employers complained that they missed out on important factors such as motivation, enthusiasm and personal characteristics; factors which perhaps matter the most when it comes to fitting into an organisation.

It's no wonder then that employers were on the lookout for an alternative that could reintroduce into the recruitment process something akin to normal human behaviour.

The answer appears to be strengths-based interviewing.

Strengths-based interviews focus not on what students *can* do, but what they *enjoy* doing; things that bring out the best in them.

Strengths-based interviews ask questions like 'What did you most enjoy doing as part of your degree course?' 'What are you best at . . . ?' 'From the following group of skills, which do you enjoy using the most?'

At the time of writing, there is a movement of recruiters away from competency and towards strengths-based interviews. Employers say that by exploring not what students can do but what they love to do, they have a chance to engage more effectively with candidates.

Task

Jot down three or four strengths-based interview questions (e.g. 'What do you really like about your current course?' 'What's been the best thing about your current module or assignment?' and see how your child gets on.

18
Assessment centres

Not all graduate jobs involve assessment centres, but if your child is applying to one of the leading UK graduate recruiters there's a good chance that an assessment centre will feature in some part of the recruitment process.

Think of assessment centres as the final stage of the graduate recruitment process – the graduate job market equivalent of finding yourself starring in your very own version of the TV show *The Apprentice*. So, if you're going to help your child to be hired, what do you need to know about assessment centres?

Rumour has it that assessment centres were first invented during the First World War by the German army, who used them for officer selection. Legend has it that the Germans used to conclude their assessment centres with bouts of electric shock treatments – whoever could cling on to a live wire for the longest had themselves a job.

You'll be pleased to hear that today's graduate recruiters have long since abandoned the use of electric shocks. But that's not to say that assessment centres are entirely pain-free.

How assessment centres work

Assessment centres are generally the final stage in the recruitment process. Get through this and you're either offered a job or turned down. Assessment centres are the FA Cup Finals of the graduate job market; the job-seeker's moment of truth.

Duration-wise, assessment centres generally last for anything between half a day and two full days. Crudely speaking, half-day assessment centres often take place with small and medium-sized firms, while large recruiters tend to opt for two days.

The format of assessment centres varies from organisation to organisation. Most, however, tend to include some aspects of the following.

- Introductory welcome presentations by members of the organisation's staff.
- Group discussions in which all candidates participate.
- Individual and/or team presentations.
- Psychometric tests (such as numeracy, literacy, and IQ tests).

- Assessed group and team exercises.
- Final candidate interviews.

Assessment centres are the organisation's final opportunity to look at candidates over a sustained period of time. Recruiters want to see how candidates perform in different situations – alone, when working in teams and small groups, when presenting to audiences, and when dealing with complex tasks and challenges. Some form of psychometric testing is often included in the form of general IQ tests designed to assess different aspects of a candidate's personal and cognitive abilities.

Usually the most daunting aspects of the assessment centre, students tell us, is the formal dinner which takes place the evening before the final day. Attending this dinner are often senior members of the organisation's management team. Accompanying them might be the selectors themselves, newly hired graduates, section heads – even guests from other partner organisations. Although ostensibly these dinners are informal, giving an opportunity for applicants to get to know the organisation and its personnel in a social, non-work context, few students find these events anything other than taxing. It's as if the pseudo-social situation of a dinner has been specially set up as yet another test – a test in which the 'rules' are for some reason harder to decode.

Assessment centres usually conclude with a final panel interview. This is when the decision about whether or not to recruit the candidate is made.

Below is the inside track on how you can help your son or daughter prepare for the challenges of the assessment centre.

Group discussions

In most assessment centres, group discussions are a core component within the programme. This is when the assessors get to see how candidates interact within groups and teams. On application forms and CVs, everyone claims to possess teamwork skills. Group discussions are a very good way of proving it.

In assessment centres, group discussions are assessed. This means that candidates are observed by recruiters, who score them against pre-set skills and competencies – hence the analogy with *The Apprentice*. Candidates are on show and competing directly with other members of their group.

This is where things get tricky. Talk to recruiters about what they expect from group discussions and they'll tell you that they want to see how graduates behave in real-life group situations. But few discussions, either in the workplace or any other social context, have such momentous and potentially life-changing results attached to them. Acting naturally is the last thing anyone is likely to do when a recruiter is sat behind them with a pencil and a clipboard.

So here's the challenge. Group discussions are to be approached as naturally as possible, while never losing sight of the fact that each member of the group is having their contribution to the discussion assessed.

With this in mind, there are several pointers worth stressing to your child before they attend an assessment centre.

Topics

The format of group discussions tends to be reasonably predictable. Within a stated time period, candidates are given a topic or subject to discuss and an objective to achieve.

Contribution counts

Remember, in an assessed environment, recruiters can only assess what people do and say. In all group discussions some people will always contribute more than others. Despite what students often think, talking too much, dominating the discussion without letting anyone else in, rarely goes down well with recruiters (after all, would you like to work with someone who hogs every interaction?). At the same time, remaining silent or failing to contribute can easily be mistaken for a lack of interest or motivation.

Positive thinking

During group discussions, students often worry about not knowing what to say. To some extent, the content of what is said is often less important than how it's said. Of course there are limits, but generally what recruiters look for is a positive contribution and a lively, interesting way of thinking. I once came across an example of a student whose only contribution in a group discussion was to say, 'I think we're going off the point,' and 'We'd better start working towards the conclusion because there's only five minutes left.' Recruiters were impressed with her task-focus and her assertiveness in the face of several very dominant characters.

Not sure what to do?

This is easy: volunteer to be the timekeeper. It might be a tried and tested tactic, but it still works! If your child is unsure about how best to make a contribution to a group discussion, encourage them to volunteer to be the timekeeper or note-taker. At the very least, it shows positive thinking, confidence and an ability to focus. Even better, it gives a less verbally confident candidate something important to do. If you can't say something memorable, do something that gets you remembered (for the right reasons).

Make sure everyone gets a say

Group discussions are stage-managed to help the recruiters see how, once in the workplace, candidates are likely to behave with their colleagues. For this reason, it's essential that your child is positive and supportive to other group members no matter how objectionable or controversial they might find them. Encourage them to be the person who makes sure everyone has had their say. Make sure they're aware of their body language.

Presentations

When selecting graduates, employers rarely pass up an opportunity to have candidates make presentations. That's because in today's workplace most graduate jobs involve giving presentations, either in teams or individually. Presentations are a powerful medium through which organisations communicate their brand values and so graduate recruits are expected to be effective presenters. What better way, then, of assessing someone's presentation skills than by asking them to present to the group?

Fortunately, when it comes to presentation skills, most degree courses now include presentations. This means that most students, regardless of their subject discipline, have had some experience of presenting to groups. Nevertheless, for most graduates, giving a presentation in a format as formal and important as an assessment centre is a daunting experience.

In terms of structure, assessment centres generally involve two types of presentations. The first type involves candidates being given a set subject to present on. This could be related to the organisation itself (another reason for encouraging them to do their background reading), or second, it could be on a subject of the candidate's own choice. Option two sounds easier – after all, it's up to you what you talk about. But too much latitude for choice can also be problematic. Where do you begin? For this reason, it's a good idea to encourage your child to think about a couple of subjects that, if required, they could give a short presentation on. Having a subject up your sleeve, no matter how rough and ready, is always better than having nothing at all.

As with group discussions, when it comes to presentation skills, the following key tips are worth stressing.

Practice

Encourage your son or daughter to take every opportunity to practise giving presentations. These don't have to be formal: standing up in front of family and friends can be just as effective when helping tackle nerves.

The power of three

One of the most common failings when candidates give presentations at assessment centres is the tendency to cram in too much information, with the result that the presentation either runs over time or key points are obliterated by a deluge of unimportant details and data. The human brain is programmed to respond best to just three key points – anything more, and things start to blur. Keep it in mind: *Tom, Dick & Harry; Best, Law & Charlton; The-Rolling-Stones; Apple-i-Pod* . . . whatever three-point rule you use, emphasise the power of three.

Where to focus

It's you that's being assessed, not your PowerPoint slides. A self-explanatory point, which graduates over-look in the rush to produce the world's greatest PowerPoint show. Remember to stress to your child that when giving presentations they should look at the audience, not the wall on which the slides are being projected. Eye contact is the ultimate sign of confidence.

Keep to time

Presentations at assessment centres are often very brief – five, ten, 15 minutes max. Recruiters also demand that presenters stick to time. In some assessment centres, once the maximum time has been reached the cut-off can be brutal. Remember, finishing within the time period is a management skill all in itself. It makes you look professional, in control and focused on the task in hand (itself another example of the power of three rule).

Team presentations

The alternative to the solo presentation is the team version. On the face of it, this can seem preferable to going solo – after all, you're not up there on stage by yourself and instead of having to carry the whole presentation, key sections can be divided up between the speakers. All this is true, but remember that this is an assessment centre and not a church hall. If your child is presenting as part of a team, it's essential that they make sure their contribution is visible and weighty enough to catch the attention of the recruiters. This isn't a nativity play where some actors do nothing more than stand on the stage and wave to the audience.

Psychometric tests

As we have seen, as the competition for graduate jobs has escalated, the number of recruiters who are turning to psychometric tests has risen dramatically. It seems that in the War for Talent, there's nothing like a psychometric test to separate the players from the spectators.

The term 'psychometric test' is a fairly generic term to describe a range of psychologically based tests. Some of these are cognitive and aimed at assessing candidates' IQ and mental abilities; others focus on assessing personality and self-motivation.

A key difference between these two types of test is that while you can fail a cognitive test, you can't 'fail' a personality test (surely a relief to anyone concerned about attracting a low personality score).

There are several reasons why employers use these tests and assessments. First, it's a useful way of assessing a candidate's suitability for a job. Employers invest incredible amounts of time and effort designing their recruitment processes and, as such, take the results from these tests seriously. Second, as a sifting mechanism, psychometric tests are a highly effective and cost-efficient way to reduce a large pool of applicants.

The question is: can candidates prepare for them?

On this, psychologists are divided. Some will argue that the whole point of a psychometric test is that it is reliable, meaning that no matter how many times a candidate takes a test their results should be broadly consistent. Any significant variation in test scores from one sitting to another indicates that somewhere something is seriously wrong with the test.

This view is, however, often contested. Some psychologists argue that practising psychometric tests can improve candidates' scores, perhaps not dramatically but enough to turn some would-be failures into scrape-over-the-line successes. Partly, this is because practice improves technique and it also reduces nerves. That means that even before the test starts, candidates are more likely to be prepared.

How can you help your child prepare for psychometric tests? There are numerous online test sites that graduates can go to to find out more about selection tests. One of the best places to start is the Graduate Prospects site: www.prospects.ac.uk

Assessed group and team exercises

Assessment centres aren't all tests, discussions and presentations. Many of them also involve group and team exercises. These can come in many formats, often resembling a cross between *Dragons' Den* and *The Krypton Factor*. Here are some key points to bear in mind.

An intellectual role

For some tasks, the challenge is intellectual – to debate a subject or issue; on other occasions, the focus is on working together as a group or team to accomplish a particular challenge. Some group discussions involve candidates working together to process lots of complex data; others take the form of role play where the group takes on the role of a senior management team whose task it is to overcome various forms of political or business-related challenge.

Show your enjoyment

Look as though you're enjoying yourself. Even if the challenge or team exercise seems trivial, make sure you encourage your child to make every attempt to join in. Recruiters are looking for graduates who are motivated and dynamic, not people who are content to sit on the sidelines rolling their eyes. Join in, participate, make a difference and, no matter how odd or lightweight the challenge, make sure the outcome is achieved.

Preparation essentials

If your child is preparing for an assessment centre, the following tips will come in handy.

- Remember that candidates are being constantly assessed. Be yourself, but never let your guard down entirely.

- Bear in mind that during their time at assessment centre, everyone your son or daughter meets from the organisation is likely to have an input in the final recruitment decision. So always be nice to receptionists!

- Presentations are a key part of assessment centres. Before attending, make sure your child has honed their presentation skills. You can do this by getting them to present in front of family and friends.

- Psychometric tests can be practised. IQ tests aren't infallible; bookshops stock lots of examples of company tests. Get hold of one and encourage your son or daughter to work through it. It will come in handy.

- Stress the importance of participation. Assessment centres are not designed to flush out future Hollywood stars. Employers want candidates to be themselves, but they also want to see them join in. If candidates keep in the background, they'll be overlooked.

- Encourage your child to do even more research on the organisation prior to attending the assessment centre.

For more advice on assessment centres, take a look at *You're Hired: Assessment Centres* (Trotman, 2011).

Task

Practise with your child the art of making small talk over dinner. It might sound ridiculous, but being able to communicate in a business/social environment is a key skill that's required by nearly all graduate recruiters.

19
Make the most of networks

As a parent, there are lots of things you can do to help your child acquire fantastic work experience, and the good news is, you don't have to rely on your child's school or college. You do it by using the power of networking.

When it comes to giving your child an advantage in the job market, nothing works quite as effectively as networks and personal contacts. Parents are a great source of largely untapped and under-utilised contacts – people who, through their advice, insights, information and knowledge can help take your child to the next level of their career planning.

Many commentators have argued that this is immoral, that the use of contacts and social networks gives some people ready-made advantages. Others, in defence of networking, claim that the use of contacts has always been a feature of the graduate job market, that in even the boom times some graduates started the journey to the job market considerably better placed than others.

This section takes a different view. I want to suggest that all graduates, regardless of their social and economic backgrounds, have access to potentially useful and valuable contacts and networks. However, in order to access these networks, they need the support of families, friends, neighbours, teachers, lecturers, employers and, above all, parents.

Like it or not, networking is where you as a parent can make the biggest impact of all.

Networking is not illegal, immoral, unethical or even particularly complicated. In fact, it approximates to normal human behaviour. Chances are you do it all the time, you just haven't realised it.

So what is it and how does it work?

Relax, it's not as bad as it sounds

For many parents, the idea of networking gives them a sinking feeling. Perhaps it's because it sounds suspiciously like speed-dating or some other form of forced social embarrassment. It could be because it sounds so contrived, so cringe-making. Fortunately, the idea is much worse than the actual reality.

Networking simply means a process where you make it your business to get to know people; people whose business, experience, insights, expertise, and support will take you a step further to your objective – whatever that objective might be. Networking can be social and it can be business; it can be formal and it can be entirely informal. Networking operates directly through human interaction. It's about establishing a set of contacts among people with whom you share common social, professional or career interests.

People think that to be a great networker you have to be a good talker. The opposite is true. The best networkers aren't always good talkers, but they are fantastic listeners. Listening is a much under-rated business and life skill. But when it comes to networking, it comes into its own.

Networking is also methodical; it's about planning who you want to meet and knowing exactly why. Don't be deceived by their apparent casual approach and nonchalant conversation; great networkers have a campaign plan as well drawn out as any military strategy. Networkers do their homework and hate to leave anything to chance.

But don't worry. There's nothing phoney to networking. In fact, a lack of authenticity is the one characteristic that's guaranteed to bring a networker crashing to earth. That's because the secret of good networking is that it's all about being genuine, projecting your own personal values, ideals, skills and personality.

Without realising it, you've probably been networking for years – perhaps it's played a major role in your own career. So why is it so effective?

Why networking works

Networking reaches parts of the job market other techniques can't reach because it's the one job search strategy that most resembles normal human behaviour. It works because of the following.

- People prefer doing business and spending time with those they know and trust.
- We're all biased towards people we know and who have similar characteristics to us.
- People generally like talking about themselves.
- Natural wariness of others makes those we trust appear extra important.
- Deep down, we all believe we're excellent judges of character.

In a job context, there's nothing new about networking. In fact, it's always existed. Its goal is to provide opportunities for gaining information from those in a particular career field. Such people don't have to be industry leaders or champions of business. They don't even need to be in managerial posts. What they do need to have is a particular insight or experience, or contact to an industry or job, in which your child is interested.

Parents and networking

As a parent, over the years, you will possibly have built up a range of contacts. Some of these you will have generated via your job or career; others will have been acquired through family, leisure and other social contexts.

If you haven't developed many contacts, don't worry. Your child's college or university is a mine of potential contacts, particularly through careers fairs and other employer-related events.

The key to building a good network is to know exactly why you need it. Having a clear objective is the best way to start networking. As a parent, your objective might be to help your child find out more information about a particular career; it could even be simply to gain a better insight into the world of work. Either way, before you start thinking about who you want to approach, you need to take time to establish what it is that you want to gain from the conversations.

The second point to remember about networking is that the more you give, the more you receive. Top-class networkers never begin conversations by asking what they can get from their contacts, but what they can give. It's not that they're unbelievably selfless and altruistic. It's because they know that the more they help their contacts to achieve their objectives, the more in turn their contacts will feel obliged to help them with theirs. It's one of life's great under-utilised facts of life that people love returning favours.

Remember, when thinking about who you can approach, you don't have to focus on only those who have worked in a relevant job or organisation; it could be that you know people who have worked in similar fields. Either way, your first task is to make a list of your contacts, trying to prioritise them according to fields such as experience, occupation, industry and access to wider networks.

Through networking you can help your child access high-quality, high-value work experience placements. You can do this by following the example of other parents and using your networking contacts to help arrange on behalf of your child, work placements, visits to organisations, work-related projects and even internships. You can even use contacts to help arrange part-time jobs.

In doing this, you will be in good company. In the past five years, growing numbers of parents have used their contacts and networks to arrange work experience placements – some have even started trading work experience placements amongst their friends. As one parent said:

> ❝ It operates like this. You take my child for a fortnight to gain work experience working in your firm, and I'll reciprocate the favour by having your son come and gain work experience with me. It's reciprocal, it's organised parent-to-parent, and it works. ❞

But the benefits of parent networking go further than setting up work placements. Your network is the ideal place to gauge future career options, to check out possible areas of job opportunities and career trends. It's the ideal place for your son or daughter to find out about the world of work by talking to people who you know. This is one reason why, for young people, tapping in to a parent's contacts and networks can be so effective. It's like having an immediate career boost.

Network building

As a parent your life experience means that straight away you have a ready-made, on-hand list of actual and potential contacts. Other parents, neighbours, colleagues at work, even members of the family, all are prospective contacts that you can tap into when setting out to develop your network. And best of all, they're probably no more than a handshake or telephone call away.

To start building a network, there are several steps that you might find useful to consider.

Recording contacts

Because networking happens across all social contexts, it is essential that you get into the habit of recording your contacts. At the very least, you need to find a way to record your contacts' details. There are numerous ways you can do this, but what matters is that your contacts' details are easily accessible (to you and your child) whenever you need them.

A contacts database can be particularly effective, even if it is just a folder containing all the business cards you have collected, as can a simple Outlook calendar. Both you and your child should get into the habit of keeping notes on when and where you met the contact and what was discussed. You never know when a contact may come in handy.

Business cards

One of the best strategies you can encourage your child to take before they look to start networking, is to get hold of a business card. Business cards are hugely underrated, particularly among students. Business cards show job-seekers to be different, professional and prepared – three essential employability qualities.

The other benefit of business cards is that no-one ever throws them away. They're also cheap. Best of all, once you hand someone your business card, it's practically impossible for them to avoid returning the compliment. Fairly soon, your child will have their own collection of business cards complete with personal telephone numbers, email addresses and job titles of key contacts. Remember: emails are deleted, CVs are shredded, addresses are lost, but business cards always get through.

And don't worry about your child's business card being too elaborate. Simple works best: name, address, telephone number, email address. Then get lots of copies made.

Informational interviewing

One of the best ways to benefit from networks is through an informational interview. This can be a very powerful way to help your child explore specific occupations or organisations. And because networking is at the heart of any informational interview, as a parent you have a unique opportunity to help set up the interview.

The idea of an informational interview is fairly simple. Instead of waiting passively for jobs and leads to appear in newspapers or online job sites, you encourage your child to take destiny in their hands and organise a brief meeting or interview with someone in your network who is either employed in, or is knowledgeable about, a career that they would like to find out more about. The meeting is structured informally around four or five questions and focused very much on uncovering information that would otherwise not be available or easy to source. Think of informational interviewing as a way of helping your child gain more information on a specific job. It's not a back-door route to employment and it's not about giving your son or daughter an unfair advantage. It's about research and information.

The four assumptions

At the heart of informational interviewing are four key assumptions.

1. If you want to help your child find out more about a job or an organisation, you can't do better than help them get to talk to someone who is currently working in that job or organisation, or who has relevant and recent experience.

2. Most people, within reason, enjoy discussing their own careers, jobs or organisations with others, particularly the children of valued contacts.

3. Most of these people, again, within reason, can spare 20 minutes, which is the maximum length of time an informational interview should take.

4. Most people in jobs and organisations are well placed to give useful advice and guidance about their job sector and industry. This advice is usually very valuable, particularly when offered freely.

How to set up an informational interview

There is nothing particularly complicated about informational interviewing: it basically equates to normal human behaviour. But if you're going to help make it as effective and useful as possible for your child, it's a good idea to observe the following rules.

*   Informational interviewing works best if you get your son or daughter to make the initial approach. No matter how well you know the contact, how much business you have done with them in the past – even if it's your best friend we're talking about – resist the urge to organise the interview. It always looks better if it's your child who is in charge, even if you're in the background.

*   Make sure your child only contacts people who are at a level that is appropriate to their skills and experience. In other words, instead of encouraging your child to speak to the CEO, aim for someone at a more commensurate level. Not only will a successful outcome be more likely but the discussion will probably be more relevant and, ultimately, useful.

*   Never ask a contact for more than 20 minutes of their time. Never ask for 'half-an-hour' – this is much too general and vague. Twenty minutes. No more, no less.

*   Repeatedly stress to your child that the aim of informational interviewing is to find out more about a job in which they might (or might not) be

interested. It's a unique and powerful opportunity to find out useful information. Think of it as a research exercise rather than an audition.

- When encouraging your child to arrange an information interview, remember that personal recommendations and introductions are worth far more than speculative letters or phone calls.

- Before the interview, make sure your child has a list of questions to ask. These questions should be genuine and designed to elicit valuable information. Courtesy is essential, and that is why using the interview to ask for a job is never a good idea.

- Before the interview finishes, stress to your child the importance of asking the following question: 'Who, in your opinion, should I go and speak to now?' This question is vital because once the contact gives your child a name, they have taken the first steps towards building their own network. From now on in, they're an insider!

- How many informational interviews your child aims to complete depends to some extent on how well the interviews are going. If they don't feel that any useful information is being generated, encourage them to stop and rethink the approach. Of course, informational interviews might also have the potentially unforeseen outcome of completely changing your child's career aspirations, putting them off a career which initially looked highly promising.

- Immediately after an informational interview make sure your child writes a personal letter of thanks to the contact. Handwritten letters are always more impressive than typed ones or, of course, emails.

20

Even the best laid plans . . . what to do if things go wrong

No matter how much you prepare, few careers go completely to plan. In today's job market, with so many graduates competing for the same jobs, the sheer law of averages predicts that at least some of your child's job applications will end in failure. So, if and when this happens, what are the points you need to bear in mind?

T housands of students every year compete for graduate jobs ... only to be rejected. At the time, the sense of disappointment can be overwhelming – more so, if they have been used to lots of academic success. *'How can I have been rejected?' 'What did I do wrong?' 'What does this mean for my future career?'*

But when it comes to the graduate job market, learning to deal with failure and rejection is a crucial employability skill – a key component within a student's self-reliance toolkit. It might sound like a line from an old cowboy film, but when it comes to graduate jobs, it's not failure that matters. It's learning how to deal with it.

Famous flunkers

The list of students who have failed either at university or in the job market, only to go on to record glittering careers, is long and impressive. Apart from founding world-changing IT empires, what else have Bill Gates and Steve Jobs got in common? Both dropped out of university.

The same goes for Hollywood actresses Sharon Stone and Andie MacDowell. Not that it seems to have flattened their career trajectories.

Even Prince William, before opting to study a degree in geography, had an unsuccessful attempt at reading history of art. Once he'd switched courses, he never looked back. From that day on, the only 'old masters' William would encounter would be toting theodolites and wearing kagouls.

But at least he was in good company. Each year, around 20,000 students switch courses or universities. Most of these transfers take place during their first year when many young people suddenly discover that their initial choice of degree subject wasn't all that well made.

Universities have long recognised that during a student's first year at university various events and issues can emerge which, if unaddressed, can prompt them to drop out or switch courses. According to a study by Universities UK, the organisation set up to represent Britain's universities, during a student's first year, five critical 'flashpoints' exist.

Critical flashpoints in a student's first year of studies

Flashpoint	When?	Why?
1	The first six to eight weeks	Chronic homesickness makes everything seem strange, unfamiliar and scary
2	The first formal assessment – if no feedback is soon forthcoming	Some students have a tendency to worry that they are not up to the grade – lack of feedback only increases these fears
3	Examination period at the end of the first semester	Poor results may rock an already low self-esteem
4	The long Christmas break leading up to the first exams	The months after Christmas can be extra gloomy times for new students: bad weather mixed with impending exams equals low motivation and dreams of escaping
5	Returning to university after the end of the first summer break	Most students now work during the long summer holidays. Giving up on a regular income can be tough, even for the most dedicated

Source: UUK

From a parent's point of view, this chart is useful because it helps you understand when, particularly during your son or daughter's first year at university, the critical 'make or break' points are to be found. Once these have been identified, it's easier to make sure the necessary support and guidance are available when your child needs it.

Flashpoints in the job market

Similar flashpoints exist within the graduate job market.

Flashpoint 1: usually takes place during a student's first or second year, when it suddenly dawns on them that time at university passes very quickly.

Flashpoint 2: often occurs at the beginning of the final year. This is the moment when students suddenly grasp how close they are to graduation . . . and to the end of university.

Flashpoint 3: usually arrives when students encounter graduate recruiters. For many, this takes place during careers fairs or recruitment seminars. For others, it might be during workshops organised by the careers service. Suddenly, students are exposed to real-life recruiters, people who they'll soon be applying to with job applications.

Flashpoint 4: comes with the realisation of how competitive the graduate job market is, how early closing dates have been set and just how difficult it is to complete job applications.

Flashpoint 5: comes with the first rejection. For many students, this is the first time that things haven't gone entirely their own way and their first encounter with the harsh realities of the world of work.

It's not personal, just business

So what should you say to a student who's just been informed by letter or by telephone that they haven't been selected for a job on which their heart was set?

As a parent, moments like these are filled with danger. Say the wrong word, sound too flippant or off-hand, and you could easily be accused of not caring. Alternatively, ranting and raving about the injustices of the job market can also lead to difficulties. After all, failure to get a job you really want happens to everyone now and again. It's the unwritten law of the labour market.

Below are some pointers that might help you if your son or daughter should be rejected by a graduate recruiter.

Don't take it personally

Not getting a job isn't a reflection of personal worth or value – it's not even a reflection of overall employability. All that's happened is that an employer has had to make a decision about which person to choose for a particular job.

Look on the bright side

If your son or daughter was rejected after attending an interview or assessment centre, console them that they were at least within touching distance of a job offer. If this has happened several times, this might be scant consolation. But at least it shows that their application form or CV is working well for them and that with a bit of practice, they should be able to succeed. Make sure after the next interview or assessment centre rejection they ask for detailed feedback.

Stay positive

After receiving a rejection letter make sure your child sends the recruiter or employer a formal letter of thanks. For maximum impact, this should always be handwritten. In it, your child should thank the organisation for taking the time to consider them for the position and ask to be considered for any future opportunities. It shows a positive attitude and that the value of courtesy can never be underestimated.

Post-match analysis

Although it's probably the last thing they feel like, spend some time with your child going over the different stages of the recruitment and selection process. Start with the CV or application form. Was it as good as it might have been? What changes could be made? Then, if relevant, think about the job interview: what went well; what didn't go to plan; and what could be done better?

Feedback

If after a job interview or assessment centre, your child has been rejected, encourage them to ask the recruiter for feedback. This could be in the form of a written summary of their performance or it could even be delivered over the telephone. What matters is that your child gets an opportunity to review their performance with a recruiter. Before the conversation takes place, make sure they're primed to ask what the employer considered were their strengths and weaknesses, and how, in the employer's view, they might improve. Employers are not obliged to provide feedback, but in my experience most are more than willing to oblige.

Look to the next opportunity

As one door closes, you can be sure that other doors are opening. All you have to do is know where to look. If your child is receiving multiple rejections, encourage them to talk to their university careers service. Most careers services offer ongoing help and support to new and recent graduates, either face to face or over the internet.

Combating under-employment

At the start of this book, the spectre of under-employment was raised. This is when graduates are employed in jobs for which degree qualifications aren't usually required. According to one study, six months after leaving university over half of all new graduates are either under-employed (working in lower-skilled jobs for which degrees aren't usually required) or they're out of work altogether. Since the economic downturn, numbers of students finding themselves in this category have been slowly rising.

For the media, graduate under-employment is always a hot topic, but in reality there's nothing much that's new about it. Even in economic boom periods, some graduates have always started their careers in non-graduate jobs. For some, this wasn't actually a choice as these were the only jobs available. For others, however, choice definitely came into play. It might sound strange, but after leaving university not all graduates want to go directly into a 'graduate' job. For some, discovering your career ambitions takes time and trial and error.

But if under-employment is to become a more prominent feature of today's job market, the Americans have a saying which is worthwhile repeating:

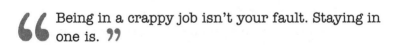 Being in a crappy job isn't your fault. Staying in one is. "

This is a powerful statement for it recognises that in a crunched job market some graduates will inevitably find themselves starting work in sub-graduate jobs. At the same time, it's a powerful call to action. Just because you begin your career in a lower-level job, who's to say that's where you have to stay?

How to run an escape committee

1. All jobs, no matter how low-level, monotonous and seemingly unimpressive, offer opportunities for acquiring and developing employability skills. You might have to look hard to find them, but trust me, they're there somewhere.

2. Don't ever let a job define you. Being a graduate isn't a job title, it's a state of mind.

3. Don't be hemmed in by jobs; see if you can design your own.

4. When appropriate, let your boss know that you're keen to develop your role. Ask for their advice.

5. Never stop looking for graduate jobs – use every network, website, careers service and careers resource you can get your hands on. Treat it as your real-life undercover job.

6. Keep your CV up to date and relevant. Have it on 24-hour stand-by.

7. At interviews, no matter how much you dislike your current job, never criticise your employer. Managers never warm to people who criticise other managers

(after all, give it a few months and it could be them whose character you're roasting). Also, you'd be mortified if it turned out you were talking about a friend of theirs.

8. Few jobs are really dead-enders. Most have concealed entrances and half-hidden escape routes. Make finding a new job your (real) job and something to which you give genuine time and commitment.

9. Keep your skills honed: evening classes, distance learning and online courses are all brilliant ways of keeping your graduate skills up to date. Just because your job doesn't call for high-level skills doesn't mean you can't be acquiring them.

10. Join the 'Escape Committee'. If the job's really not for you, set yourself a date by which you'll have left. Focusing on a particular date will help you avoid becoming acclimatised to the environment, which is the main reason so many people stay in jobs they hate.

Employability timeline

Here is a timeline for how you and your child can use all this information to put together a viable plan of action. But first, a brief word about timelines.

When it comes to career planning, timelines can be useful in showing you how things fit together. What they don't convey, however, is real life. Few people's careers follow 'ideal' patterns or timescales. Instead, they're influenced and shaped by the unforeseen, the unexpected and even, at times, the unwanted. Take age, for example. Once, most students entering university were 18 or 19 years old. Today, on enrolment, students' ages are far more varied, with many choosing to go to university much later in their lives. Nevertheless, if used with caution, a timeline can be useful in helping you and your child plan the next few years.

On the opposite page is a standard timeline showing how an idealised student's career planning might look like. Notice in particular where work experience, extra-curricular activities and other 'informal' events come in.

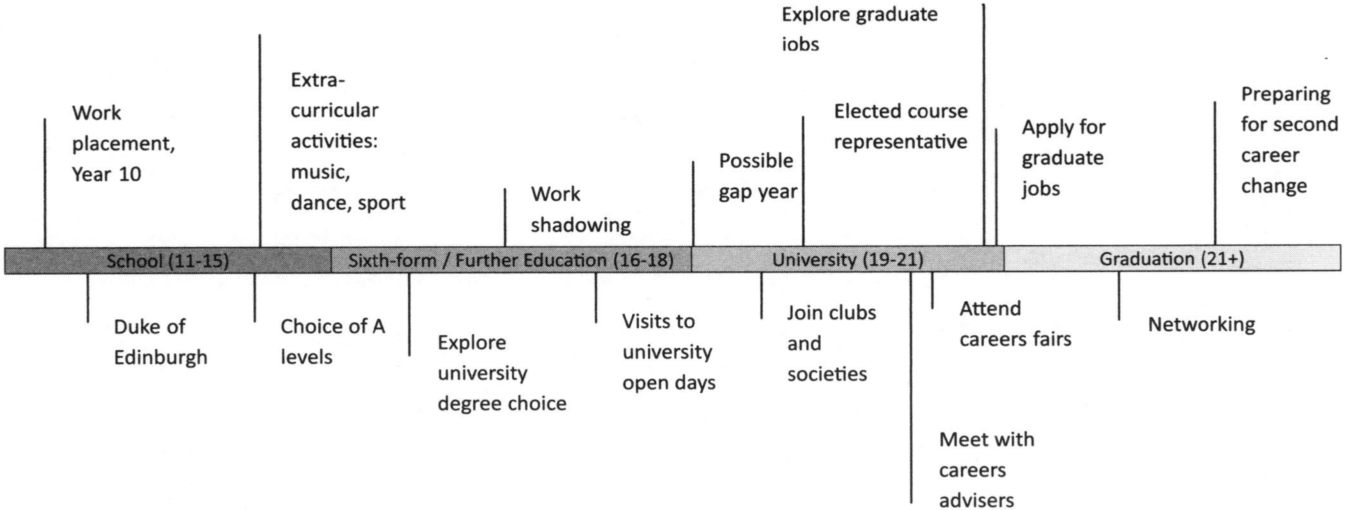
School (11-15)
Sixth-form / Further Education (16-18)
University (19-21)
Graduation (21+)
Work placement, Year 10
Duke of Edinburgh
Extra-curricular activities: music, dance, sport
Choice of A levels
Explore university degree choice
Work shadowing
Visits to university open days
Possible gap year
Join clubs and societies
Elected course representative
Explore graduate iobs
Meet with careers advisers
Attend careers fairs
Apply for graduate jobs
Networking
Preparing for second career change

Conclusion

This book began with an overview of just how difficult today's graduate job market is. Yet hopefully what the book will have also conveyed to you and your child is that despite the increased competition, the graduate job market is still very much open for business.

Getting a degree is still the best career option – both now and in the long-term.

That doesn't mean to say that there's any room for complacency. In your career you've probably had to compete with people from your own town, city or country. In your child's career, the competition will be global. The challenge of becoming and remaining employable will never be greater.

As a parent, your role in your child's employability is destined to become even more important. Once, parents had limited impact on their child's career, particularly once they had enrolled at university.

In today's job market and in today's world of work, the supportive role of a parent is only just beginning . . .

My research into the role of parents in today's graduate job market has led me to draw the following conclusions. If you want to use your role as parent effectively the following ground rules have got to apply.

1. Be clear about how far you're willing to go to help your child – draw up boundaries and make sure you both stick to them.

2. Focus on those parts of the career search process that you're both good at and keep to them. Ask

yourself what is it that both you and your child contribute that's unique and special?

3. Remember, it's their career not yours and never seek to realise your own career ambitions through your child.

4. No matter how much you help your child get a job, they call the shots. No matter how frustrating, it's their speed you travel at.

5. When it comes to the graduate job market, assume nothing and never think you know best. With the world of work changing so fast, you almost certainly don't.

6. Never take any action that's not totally above board. It's not your career you're putting at risk, but theirs.

7. State your point of view clearly and concisely but don't be offended when your child rejects it. After all, it's not personal, just business.

8. Never talk to anyone on your child's behalf. Your task is to make sure they have the skill, confidence and self-assurance to go it alone.

9. Don't lean on anyone on their behalf, no matter how tempting. Putting pressure on people has a habit of rebounding in ways that are as unpredictable as they are unwelcome.

10. Learn how to fade gracefully into the background. Remember, your role as a parent is to be the consigliere, not the Don.

Glossary

AGCAS	Association of Graduate Careers Advisory Services.
AGR	Association of Graduate Recruiters – the organisation responsible for representing and promoting the UK's leading graduate recruiters.
Child	For the purposes of this book, your 'child' can be assumed to be of any age, height, marital status and level of education.
DLHE	Destination of Leavers from Higher Education – the biggest, most comprehensive annual survey of what graduates do in the first six months after leaving university. Undertaken by university careers services.
Graduate	A generic term used throughout the book to indicate a student who has completed a university course or programme. In most cases, a 'graduate' will have completed a first (i.e. undergraduate) degree.
Employability	The ability to be able to move between jobs and careers, making your own decisions, calling your own shots, deciding your own fate. Employability is to employment what a one-off fish supper is to acquiring the skills and knowledge to be able to fish.
HECSU	Higher Education Careers Service Unit – one of the UK's largest publishers of graduate careers vacancies and material.

HEFCE	The Higher Education Funding Council for England – the official organisation responsible for funding, promoting and paying for the country's higher education institutions.
HESA	The Higher Education Statistics Agency – the government body responsible for providing statistical data on higher education.
Helicopter parent	Term for an over-protective, ever-hovering parent. Particularly prevalent at careers fairs, graduate recruitment events and university open days. Can be highly effective, once boundaries have been negotiated.
Internship	A period of work experience, usually undertaken by a graduate who has already completed their studies. Controversy currently surrounds whether internships should be paid or not.
Parent	Used in its widest sense, 'parents' in this book can be uncles, aunts, grandparents, guardians, distant relatives, siblings, step-parents and of course, actual mums and dads.
Russell Group	The top 20 or so leading research-intensive universities (Britain's equivalent of the American Ivy League).
Student	A student is currently enrolled in either further or higher education.
University	In the UK, universities are essentially institutions of higher education that can give out degree qualifications. Some focus more on teaching; others on research and high-level scholarship.
Under-employment	Working in a job for which one is over-qualified.

Further reading

Career Coach, Corinne Mills (Trotman, 2011)

The Graduate Jobs Formula, Paul Redmond (Trotman, 2010)

What do graduates do?, The Association of Graduate Careers Advisory Services (Higher Education Careers Service Unit)

What Employers Want, Karen Holmes (Trotman, 2011)

You're Hired! Assessment Centres, Ceri Roderick (Trotman, 2011)

You're Hired! CVs, Interviews and Psychometric Tests, James Meachin, Ceri Roderick, Corinne Mills and Stephen Lucks (Trotman, 2011)

You're Hired! Interview, Judi James (Trotman, 2009)